GCSE
Citizenship Studies
Exam Techniques

a 15-week revision programme

Peter Brett
A GCSE Citizenship Studies Chair of Examiners

Acknowledgements

pp. 7, 10 *National Curriculum KS4*
pp. 12–13 Professor Ted Wragg, © *Guardian*
p.15 Citizenship Foundation
p.17 Ben Summerskill © *Observer*
pp.18–19 © Phillipa Budgen, 31, 33, 69, 70 © *Guardian*
pp.21–22, 28, 35 © *Observer*
pp.44–45 The National Youth Agency and the Citizenship Foundation
p.65 *Education for Citizenship and the Teaching of Democracy in Schools*
pp.67–68 Hansard Society
p.71 Channel 4
p.75 © Guardian
p.84 Victim Support

United Kingdom: Folens Publishers, Apex Business Centre, Boscombe Road, Dunstable, LU5 4RL.
Email: folens@folens.com

Ireland: Folens Publishers, Greenhills Road, Tallaght, Dublin 24.
Email: info@folens.ie

Poland: JUKA, ul. Renesansowa 38, Warsaw 01-905

Editor: Dawn Booth
Layout artist: Suzanne Ward
Illustrations: Dave Thompson
Cover design: Martin Cross/2i Design

First published 2004 by Folens Limited.

British Library Cataloguing in Publication Data. A catalogue record for this publication is available from the British Library.

ISBN 1-84303-018-7

Contents

Introduction	Your Questions Answered	4
Unit 1	How do I Use this Book? – A Checklist	5
Unit 2	Knowing the Papers	6
Unit 3	Key Concepts for Citizenship Studies	10
Unit 4	Revising Reading Skills	16
Unit 5	Citizenship Issues in the News	24
Unit 6	Using and Interpreting Statistics	30
Unit 7	Citizenship in Action: How to Plan, Research and Evaluate it	38
Unit 8	Structuring your Extended Writing on Citizenship Themes	46
Unit 9	Writing to Argue	54
Unit 10	Revising Local Citizenship	60
Unit 11	Revising National Citizenship	65
Unit 12	Revising Global Citizenship	71
Unit 13	Citizenship and the Law	78
Unit 14	Citizenship Studies Links with Other Subject Areas	86
Unit 15	Final Revision for Citizenship Studies	92

Introduction

Your questions answered.

Q What is the point of this book?

A The aims of this book are:
- to give a *clear insight* into the knowledge, skills and understanding you need to succeed in GCSE Citizenship Studies exams and coursework
- to show *when* and *where* those skills need to be demonstrated
- to enable you to *practise* those skills, and give you the opportunity to *develop* them *on your own*
- to *explain* how your work is *marked* by examiners
- to *provide* a *structured revision programme* building on your classwork and active Citizenship project work

   and, most important of all,

- to enable *you to gain those extra marks* which will improve your chance of *a higher grade*.

Q Does this book help me with my particular Citizenship Studies GCSE course?

A Across the units in this book there will be coverage of all possible aspects of the GCSE examination boards' specified Citizenship content and the key stage 4 Citizenship programme of study (on which all the boards have to base their courses and exams on).

Q How can this book help me get a better grade, then?

A You could work through the book, unit by unit. However, you might prefer to be more selective in developing your understanding of different aspects of the GCSE Citizenship Studies course. Look at the Checklist in Unit 1 – you might focus on key pages or sections which you, or your teacher, consider to be problematic. As you will see, the book has a clear structure which is designed to be easy to follow.

Q So, how is this revision book structured?

A There are 15 units (including the Unit 1 Checklist) which could fit the 15 weeks before your exam. Each one deals with a key aspect of the Citizenship Studies exam, whether it's *'Key Concepts for Citizenship Studies'* or *'Citizenship Issues in the News'*. Each unit is from four to nine pages long.
- An opening section will give advice and information.
- The text is divided between skills with examples and tasks that provide opportunities for more developed writing or extension work.

Q Is there anything else to help me?

A Yes. On many pages there are Examiner's Tips and reminders – that is, key pointers to help you improve your work. Also each unit ends with a summary of the main points covered.

Q Sounds great. When can I get started?

A That's easy – just begin with the Checklist opposite.

Peter Brett

Unit 1 *How do I Use this Book?*
A Checklist

Target To identify the Citizenship Studies knowledge, skills and revision areas that you need to focus on.

Do you know?	YES	NO	GO TO UNIT
● The date and time of your Citizenship Studies examination.			–
● What the examination involves (for example which examination board, how long, etc.).			2 & 15
● How your Citizenship Studies coursework relates to the examination.			7
Have you?			
● Learned how to divide up your time in the examination.			15
● Put together a palette of appropriate words for different Citizenship topics.			3, 5, 10–15
● Learned most of the key Citizenship Studies words and concepts.			3
● Practised note-taking and re-organising your Citizenship notes.			4
● Practised comparing texts, sources and documents.			5
● Understood what 'active citizenship' might mean on a local, national, and international level.			10–12
Can you?			
● Plan an essay quickly and effectively.			8–9
● Understand and analyse statistics.			6
● Interpret news stories.			5
● Argue effectively.			9
● Make links between Citizenship and other subject areas.			14
● See the relationship between the law and Citizenship.			13
Finally …			
● Do you know what makes the difference between one grade and another?			3–15

The icons, symbols and reminders – 'Focus', 'Examiner's Summary' and 'Remember' are there to emphasise the key things that you need to remember. They look like this:

FOCUS

Examiner's Summary

Remember:

Unit 2 *Knowing the Papers*

Targets

1. To understand the form of the examination.
2. To know what is tested in the Citizenship Studies examination paper.

General Information

Citizenship Studies is a relatively new short-course GCSE subject. There are three different examination boards: AQA, Edexcel and OCR, each of whom organises its courses differently, but this book is designed to help you tackle *any* of the Citizenship Studies' GCSE examinations. Find out which board/syllabus your school or college is entering you for.

Citizenship Studies GCSE

Coursework: 40% of final mark

Examinations: 60% of final mark

One examination paper: usually lasts for 1 hour 30 minutes

The Citizenship examination asks you to draw upon what you have learned in your Citizenship Studies coursework and reflect upon, for example, your:

● participation in a Citizenship activity in your school or community
● planning that has been undertaken as part of this activity
● evaluation of how successful the activity or project was.

You will find more help in this area in Units 7 and 10.

What you need for your Citizenship Studies examination

1. Double-check when and where the examination takes place.
2. Pens (take spares), pencils and a ruler in a transparent bag or case.

Dictionaries are not allowed.

You will be tested on a range of skills and, to do well, you need to be aware of:
● what is being tested
● what the examiner is looking for
● how to produce the best answers.

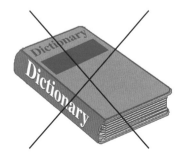

Citizenship Studies: What is being tested?

All Citizenship Studies GCSE examinations must meet the requirements of the National Curriculum programme of study for Citizenship at key stage 4 in England so it is worth reminding yourself what this is:

The Citizenship National Curriculum Programme of Study at Key Stage 4

KNOWLEDGE AND UNDERSTANDING ABOUT BECOMING INFORMED CITIZENS

1. Pupils should be taught about:
   - **a)** The legal human rights and responsibilities underpinning society and how they relate to citizens, including the role and operation of the criminal and civil justice systems.
   - **b)** The origins and implications of the diverse national, regional, religious and ethnic identities in the United Kingdom and the need for mutual respect and understanding.
   - **c)** The work of Parliament, the Government and the Courts in making and shaping the law.
   - **d)** The importance of playing an active part in democratic and electoral processes.
   - **e)** How the economy functions, including the role of business and financial services.
   - **f)** The opportunities for individuals and voluntary groups to bring about social change locally, nationally, in Europe, and internationally.
   - **g)** The importance of a free press, and the media's role in society, including the Internet, in providing information and affecting opinion.
   - **h)** The rights and responsibilities of consumers, employers and employees.
   - **i)** The United Kingdom's relations with Europe, including the European Union, and relations with the Commonwealth and the United Nations.
   - **j)** The wider issues and challenges of global interdependence and responsibility, including sustainable development and Local Agenda 21.

DEVELOPING SKILLS OF ENQUIRY AND COMMUNICATION

2. Pupils should be taught to:
   - **a)** Research a topical political, spiritual, moral, social or cultural issue, problem or event by analysing information from different sources, including ICT-based sources, showing an awareness of the use and abuse of statistics.
   - **b)** Express, justify and defend orally and in writing a personal opinion about such issues, problems or events.
   - **c)** Contribute to group and exploratory class discussions, and take part in formal debates.

DEVELOPING SKILLS OF PARTICIPATION AND RESPONSIBLE ACTION

3. Pupils should be taught to:
   - **a)** Use their imagination to consider other peoples' experiences and be able to think about, express, explain and critically evaluate views that are not their own.
   - **b)** Negotiate, decide and take part responsibly in school- and community-based activities.
   - **c)** Reflect on the process of participating.

[The Citizenship National Curriculum KS4]

Task 1

Look at the key stage 4 Citizenship National Curriculum and identify the areas where you feel confident and the topics where you feel less well informed. When you have identified the gaps in your knowledge, give priority to these areas when looking through the revision units in this book.

Other Citizenship Studies examination requirements

All Citizenship Studies GCSE examinations will give you opportunities to:

a) develop and apply knowledge and understanding about becoming informed citizens through and alongside the development of skills of enquiry, communication, participation and responsible action

b) explore local, national and international issues, problems, and events of current interest

c) critically evaluate your participation within school and/or community activities.

There are three main aims or Assessment Objectives (AOs), which are all assessed broadly equally across the examination and coursework. In your Citizenship Studies examinations you will need to:

AO1. Show your knowledge and understanding of: current affairs; roles, rights and responsibilities; communities and identities; democracy and government, and relate this appropriately to individual, local, national, and global contexts.

AO2. Obtain, explain and interpret different kinds of information, including from the media, in order to discuss, form and express an opinion formally, and in writing, and demonstrate your ability to analyse and present evidence on a variety of issues, problems and events.

AO3. Plan and evaluate the citizenship activities in which you have participated and demonstrate an understanding of your own contribution to them as well as recognising the views, experiences and contributions of others.

FOCUS
◆ *Apply knowledge and understanding on the key Citizenship topic areas.*
◆ *Apply skills of interpretation and analysis in relation to local, national, and international issues.*
◆ *Participation and reflection.*

Task 2

Read through the above information and look again at the Citizenship key stage 4 National Curriculum.

a) Name six areas where you will need to *know* and revise key information and concepts.

b) List five *skills* that you will need to demonstrate in a Citizenship Studies examination.

The structure of the Citizenship Studies examination papers

Again, you need to check which board's examination you are taking – AQA, Edexcel or OCR. There are some differences in the way in which the papers are organised but a 'typical' pattern for the questions is:

● **Section A:** A series of ten to fifteen short-answer and/or multiple-choice questions worth one or two marks each covering the whole of the course content (this is part of Section C on the Edexcel paper).

- **Section B:** Medium-length answer questions based on data that may consist of written material and/or graphs, graphics, photographs, pictures, etc. The topics will vary: examples include, the criminal justice system, asylum seekers, and analysis of a local news story. You will need to demonstrate your understanding of source material *and* use your own knowledge. (With the OCR board the sources will all relate to a defined subject area, which you will know about in advance of the examination.)
- **Section C:** An extended answer on one question chosen from one of three themes (for example, The Human Rights Act and the legal rights and responsibilities of UK citizens; the influence of the media in the UK).

On each of the examination papers you will also be required to evaluate the citizenship activities in which you have taken part and demonstrate an understanding of them as well as recognising the views, experiences and contributions of others. For Edexcel this is in Section A of the paper; for OCR and AQA this appears within Section C.

How are the marks divided up?

Look closely at how the marks are divided between the different sections of the examination paper. You will find that there is a fairly equal split between the three or four sections of the examination paper and you are advised to split your time accordingly.

AQA – four sections: 120 marks
Edexcel – three sections: 80 marks
OCR – three sections: 60 marks

Minutes = Marks
EXAMINER'S TIP!

A good general rule of thumb is to spend a minute for each mark. So, if four marks are available, spend 4 minutes on that part of the question; if 30 marks are available devote 30 minutes to the question.

FOCUS
Accurate spelling, punctuation and grammar help you gain extra marks.

You will be awarded from four to six extra marks for the quality of your written work, including spelling, punctuation, and grammar. Try not to spell key words incorrectly.

Examiner's Summary
- Find out which examination board you have been entered for and look at a past paper.
- Notice how many marks are available for different sections and questions and divide your time accordingly.

Unit 3 Key Concepts for Citizenship Studies

Targets

1. To begin to define Citizenship Studies.
2. To understand and use the language of Citizenship.
3. To learn how to respond to short Citizenship-related questions.

Skill 1: Defining Citizenship

Defining Citizenship Studies is not easy, although it is important if you want to achieve good grades. If you can sort out a definition of what Citizenship means then that is half the battle. One thing that makes the subject a bit different is that it is also important to 'do' Citizenship; it is not purely the learning of a series of dry and unrelated facts.

The Importance of Citizenship

Citizenship gives pupils the knowledge, skills and understanding to play an effective role in society at local, national, and international levels. It helps them to become informed, thoughtful and responsible citizens who are aware of their duties and rights. It promotes their spiritual, moral, social and cultural development, making them more self-confident and responsible both in and beyond the classroom. It encourages pupils to play a helpful part in the life of their schools, neighbourhoods, communities, and the wider world. It also teaches them about our economy and democratic institutions and values, encourages respect for different national religious and ethnic identities and develops pupils' ability to reflect on issues and take part in discussions. [Introductory statement]

[Introductory statement, *The Citizenship National Curriculum KS4*.]

Task 1

You probably did an exercise like this at the beginning of your course but it is an area worth revisiting.

Using the above definition of Citizenship, the Citizenship vocabulary palette on the facing page and your own knowledge, write two different statements – of between six and ten lines – that explain something about being a citizen. Start each statement in the following way:

a) A citizen is …

b) A good citizen is …

Skill 2: Understanding the language of Citizenship

You will need to show that you understand social and political issues as they appear, for example, in newspapers or magazines, and be able to follow an argument. There are key words and concepts in Citizenship that it is essential to engage with and you will need the correct vocabulary to express your ideas and queries.

Citizenship vocabulary palette

Human Rights   Identity   Tolerance   Participation   Politics   Responsibilities
Fairness   Government   Society   Prejudice   Freedom   Democracy   Parliament
Rule of Law   Community   Power   Equality   Election   Protest   Justice

---

Task 2

a) **Choose six words** that you do not understand or would find it hard to define and find out what they mean.
b) **Write six sentences**, including one of these words in each, to show how you can use your six words accurately and effectively. (Try to write an extra sentence for each word to develop your definition.)

For example: In Britain we have *freedom* of speech, which means that we are able to say what we think, including criticising the way that the country is run. However, there are legal limits to this *freedom*, for example, we are not allowed to slander or racially abuse people.

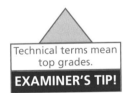

USE: A dictionary, classmate or ask a teacher.

Technical terms mean top grades.
EXAMINER'S TIP!

Revise technical terms the week before the Citizenship examination paper. Used correctly, they will impress the examiner.

Skill 3: Building up 'topic' vocabulary palettes

You may find it helpful to build upon the following word bank of useful Citizenship words, phrases, concepts, and names of organisations (p.12). Again, look up the meaning of any that you are unsure about.

Vocabulary palette: global citizenship

Developing countries   United Nations   Fair trade   Disaster relief

Sustainable development   Climate change   Global village   International aid

Multinational companies   Third-world debt   Interdependence   Epidemics

World Trade Organisation   Global inequality   Participation   Exploitation

---

Task 3

Try compiling your own palettes of at least 12 key words, similar to the example above, for the following topics:

a) The role of the media.
b) The criminal and civil justice system.

You should be able to add more words to these palettes after you have studied Units 5 and 13.

The invisible palette.

EXAMINER'S TIP!

In the examination you may not have time to draw a palette, but jot down key words and phrases, as if from an imaginary palette, ready to 'paint' on to your Citizenship essays.

Skill 4: Explaining key words in examination answers

You will probably face some shorter questions which test your understanding of key words (and will be worth one or two marks).
For example: What is meant by the term *discrimination*? (*Two marks*)
When might a *referendum* be held in Britain? (*Two marks*)

Source A: How will schools tackle the challenge of turning our students into citizens?

A few years ago I was a member of a Commission on Citizenship. There were conflicting views from witnesses about what a Citizenship programme should contain. For some it was two years in the army and a shorn head, for others a few lectures on how to claim benefits. 'Aristotle (an Ancient Greek philosopher), by contrast, saw it as a reciprocal process, stating: A citizen is one who has a share in both ruling and being ruled.'

We adopted the definition of T.H. Marshall in his 1950 book *Citizenship and Social Class*. He saw citizenship as a process with three elements: the civil (liberty, freedom of speech), the political (participating in the exercise of power), and the social (economic welfare and security, sharing a heritage). Given these noble aspirations, becoming a citizen should lie at the heart of education.

continued...

Certain aspects will be better implemented than others. The notion of 'active citizenship', for example, is attractive to many young people. The desire to avoid previous generations' cock-ups is a notable feature of adolescence. Many young people join a great cause during this period – a religion, a pressure group, a movement. The art of teaching *active citizenship* is to channel that huge potential energy into something positive.

One strand of the new citizenship curriculum is a potential disaster. 'Political literacy' will be a huge turn-off if it involves boring lectures on the history of the Labour party, or how local councils work … [Young people are] more likely to be interested in *pressure groups*, such as Amnesty International, than *party politics*. When asked: 'Do you think people of your age know much about politics?', one 15-year-old replied: 'Only the ones who haven't got a life.' … Unless *political literacy* is taught in an engaging way, it will be wasted on young people who think politicians are crooks. Those who do not understand the use and misuse of power in our society will soon become victims of it.

I just hope no-one is so foolish as to believe that pupils who do well in citizenship exams will naturally be good citizens, or indeed the reverse: that those who do less well are likely to spend their days shoplifting and nicking hubcaps …

The real test of what schools can achieve … will be what happens in about 100,000 secondary schools from September 2002 and whether much of it eventually makes any significant impact for good on people's lives.

[Abridged and adapted from an article by Professor Ted Wragg, the *Guardian*, 6 August 2002]

Task 4

Read the article above and answer the following short-answer questions.

a) **State what is meant by the term** *party politics*. (*One mark*)
b) **State one way in which a pressure group is different from a political party**. (*One mark*)
c) **Give one example of a pressure group.** (*One mark*)
d) **What do you think is meant by the term political literacy?** (*Two marks*)
e) 'A citizen is one who has a share in both ruling and being ruled.' [Aristotle] **Give two examples** of how British people have a share in ruling the country and **two examples** of how they have a share in being ruled. (*Four marks*)
f) **Choose four words** which you think best describe the opinion of the author towards the teaching of Citizenship in English schools. (*Four marks*)

Skill 5: Answering multiple-choice questions

Some of the examination boards will ask you multiple-choice questions to test your understanding of key words or concepts. You may be asked to put a ring around the number of the definition (1, 2, 3, or 4) that matches the term. Two pieces of advice here :

1. Imagine that this is like the game-show *Who Wants to be a Millionaire*? The tactics are the same, although unfortunately in an examination you cannot phone a friend or ask the audience. In other words, discard the answers that are obviously wrong. You will find that you can usually bring it down to a choice of two possible options. Then, if you are not sure, you may have to gamble but at least you have mentally taken the 50:50 option.
2. Check that you have ringed the answer that you intended to pick. This may appear to be obvious but there is nothing more annoying than knowing the answer yet losing a mark through a slip of the pen or a brief loss of concentration.

Task 5

a) **What is meant by the term devolution?**

1. The overthrow of a state or radical change.
2. More power being taken by central government from local government.
3. Scotland, Wales and Ireland made completely independent from England.
4. The transfer of some powers from central government to local, regional or national assemblies.

b) **What is meant by the term censorship?**

1. A preparedness to treat other people with respect and kindness.
2. Freedom to publish information in newspapers.
3. Forced legal limits on freedom of expression in the media.
4. Official reprimand from the police force.

c) **Local Agenda 21 is:**

1. A form to register to vote at local elections.
2. A law that compels local councils to explain how they decide on Council Tax rates.
3. A principle of acting locally while thinking globally that aims to create a society that does not destroy the earth or exploit developing countries.
4. An organisation concerned with local facilities for young people.

(Answers at the end of this unit.)

Extension work: key concepts and essay writing.

Skill 6: Reflecting on 'active citizenship'

You will have had an opportunity as part of your course to do some kind of project work in relation to your school or local community. Perhaps you have worked with others to bring about a change; this is 'active citizenship'. Read what the author of the newspaper article (Source A, pp.12–13) has to say about this concept and then study the extracts below:

> **Extract 1**: 'Ask not what your country can do for you, but what you can do for your country.'
> *[President John F. Kennedy, Inaugural Presidential Speech, January 1961]*
>
> **Extract 2**: 'Healthy democracies need well-informed citizens who take an active interest in their community. They need people who value themselves and others and who are aware of the contribution they can make to society.'
> [Citizenship Foundation website, April 2001]

Task 6

Write an essay which answers the following two questions:

Why do healthy democracies need active citizens?
Should all young people be required to do some kind of voluntary work?

To help you to structure your answers you should:

- Describe the benefits of active citizenship. (Use the extracts above as well as your own experiences to help you.)
- Give examples of positive community projects or campaigns in your area.
- Describe the difficulties of being an active citizen and why some people cannot be bothered.
- Think about the consequences if everyone was (a) a passive and (b) an inactive citizen.
- List the advantages and disadvantages of making it compulsory for young people to undertake voluntary work.
- Sum up your case. Why is active citizenship healthy for democracy?

There is more advice in Units 8 and 9 on how to structure essays and extended writing.

Answers to Task 4: a) 4; b) 3; c) 3

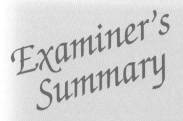
Examiner's Summary

- Identify and build up a vocabulary palette of key Citizenship words and concepts.
- Practise thinking of *examples* which will help you to *develop* your definitions of difficult words and concepts.
- Break down complicated questions into smaller sub-questions. (See the example here on active citizenship.)
- Think about how active citizenship benefits society.

Unit 4 *Revising Reading Skills*

Targets
1. To consolidate your understanding of what is tested.
2. To read text and questions carefully.
3. To practise note-taking skills.

Part of your examination will ask you to analyse written source material. This could be news articles or press releases, or it might include bullet-pointed lists, letters, advertisements or quotations from individuals or organisations. You will also have to absorb quite a lot of reading for your coursework project. It is therefore important that you read with a purpose and approach your reading in a structured and organised way.

Note: *Written material might be described in the examination paper as either 'documents' or 'sources'.*

Skill 1: Taking notes

Try making notes in a 'spidergram', 'spray' diagram or flowchart rather than continuous text. Some may prefer to use bullet points or underlining. Note-taking styles are different for different people – your notes need to help you remember things, so re-arrange material to suit you.

FOCUS
Making effective notes

Revision can be off-putting if you face pages of handwriting where you have to spend a lot of time working out the main points because they are buried in the dense text. Your notes need to let you 'see the wood for the trees'. Don't get so swamped with information that you can't see the broader issues. 'Skeleton' notes will need to be fleshed out with detail and examples but your notes will have helped to highlight the main points.

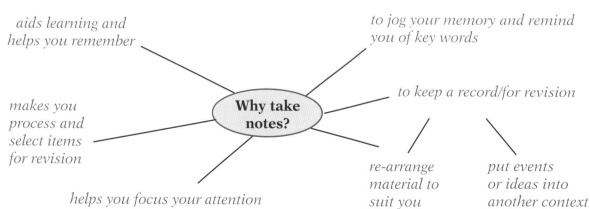

aids learning and helps you remember

to jog your memory and remind you of key words

makes you process and select items for revision

Why take notes?

to keep a record/for revision

helps you focus your attention

re-arrange material to suit you

put events or ideas into another context

Task 1

Read the article below and make notes of some of the key facts and opinions in it.

Choose your own way of organising your notes so that they make sense to you.

Source A: Government turns to children for answers

A team of 30 young people has been recruited to give advice to government on young Britain. At a first meeting with a Minister scheduled to take place next week the 11–18-year-olds will offer ideas on schools, crime and runaways. The Children and Young Persons Advisory Forum has been set up by civil servants working for a cabinet committee. Eleven departments have been asked to produce action plans on young people's issues by April 2003.

Akosua Bonsu, 15, from London commented, 'I don't think the Internet will solve any of the problems of young people not being interested in politics if politicians haven't made themselves interesting in the first place'. At the last election, more than 50% of 18–24-year-olds did not vote.

John Clarke, 13, from Staffordshire said, '… neither young people nor disabled people have a proper voice in government … Disabled people should automatically be provided with facilities such as ramps and toilets.

John McKie, a former editor of *Smash Hits* said: 'Children certainly don't take guidance from MPs any more on things such as sex and drugs, but MPs might have a lot to learn from them.'

Andy Parfitt, the controller of Radio 1, said: 'It's about getting underneath the surface and that will only happen here if the Government is genuine. You have to be committed to making more than superficial gestures. When we talk to our audience they have passionately strong views about issues like transport, the environment and street crime.

[Adapted and abridged from *Ben Summerskill*, '*Blair turns to children*', the *Observer*, 13 January 2002]

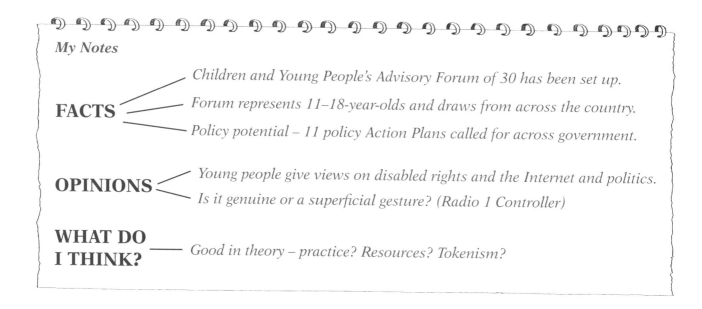

My Notes

FACTS — Children and Young People's Advisory Forum of 30 has been set up.

— Forum represents 11–18-year-olds and draws from across the country.

— Policy potential – 11 policy Action Plans called for across government.

OPINIONS — Young people give views on disabled rights and the Internet and politics.

— Is it genuine or a superficial gesture? (Radio 1 Controller)

WHAT DO I THINK? — Good in theory – practice? Resources? Tokenism?

Skill 2: What is tested in examination questions using sources?

The style of questions varies slightly from year to year but you will be expected to:

- Follow an argument – for example, read through some text and show that you understand what it is saying.
- Select appropriate material – in other words, digest your reading, put relevant points into answers and sometimes quote some words, phrases or sentences.
- Offer an informed opinion on your reading – in other words, cross-reference your own knowledge with what you read in the sources.

Some questions will be based upon your understanding of one source or document while others will ask you to look at several sources and draw conclusions.

> **Remember:** When attempting the questions in this unit, think about how you can use your own knowledge to gain higher marks.

Source B: Offenders reformed by victims – new method proves effective in changing criminals' lives

'I thought they were animals to start off with but after you've spoken to them, you feel a bit different.' The speaker is a victim of crime, talking after a face-to-face meeting with the perpetrator. A recent Home Office research project encourages young offenders to face up to the harm they have done. Tears are a regular feature of the meetings. So, too, are promises from offenders that they will change their ways, which often means sorting out a drugs problem. Victims hope that they will feel more involved in the criminal justice system and that it helps them get over the crime itself.

continued ...

Re-offending is the big issue. Statistically most young offenders re-offend within two years. Incredibly, the figure can be as high as 89% for 15–16-year-olds. For years this has got worse because there has been no system to change the ways of young criminals. Imprisonment punishes them, but rarely reforms them. A recent Australian study has shown a 38% reduction in re-offending where violent offenders met their victims. Since 1998, Thames Valley police have been testing whether so-called 'restorative' justice works for minor offences. In almost 2,000 cases the traditional police caution was replaced by a meeting of everyone affected.

Before meetings, a trained mediator checks that the offender is genuine, and is prepared for the possible reaction of the victim. The victim is also prepared for the meeting, making sure that they have realistic expectations. An evaluation of the project has been encouraging. Fifty-six young offenders were monitored and found to be half as likely to be convicted or cautioned for further offences in the following 12 months, compared to previous methods of cautioning. For most victims in the study the meeting was also a positive experience.

PC Dove, a mediator with the Thames Valley force, accepts that many young people are reluctant to meet their victims: 'They can be inarticulate and lacking the social skills required for effective dialogue with the victim.' But overall he praised the scheme: 'Youngsters have to take some responsibility for what they have done. Put simply: many kids, when they get to know the person they have hurt, realise the error of their ways. This project is helping to put some youngsters' lives back on the straight and narrow.'

[Based on statistics and case studies in Phillipa Budgen, 'Let's face it', the *Guardian*, 17 July 2002]

Task 2

Answer the following questions.

a) What details in the above report prove that the scheme has been successful? *(Four marks)*

The important words here are *details, prove* and *successful*. Prove must be related to facts. Here, the statistics help to prove the writer's point.

Write down four facts to answer this question.

FOCUS
How to get marks

b) What does the article indicate was wrong with the old system and how does it show that the new one is more successful? *(Four marks)*

The important words here are *indicate, wrong with the old system, how, show* and *new one more successful*.

This is a more difficult question and has two parts. Find and explain four things that were wrong with the old system and four reasons given to show that the new one is better.

c) Explain what some of the problems with this scheme might be? (*Four marks*)

'Explain, means you should not just be copying. When you explain, you make sense of something for the reader. You can also give your opinion.

Consider the mark scheme for questions a), b) and c).

For **Task a)** you might have mentioned the following:
● Statistically most young offenders re-offend within two years.
● The figure can be as high as 89% for 15–16-year-olds.
● An Australian study has shown a 38% reduction.

For **Task b)** you might have included the following:
● Figures for re-offending have been too high ('incredibly').
● There has been no system to change criminals' ways.
● Prison only punishes criminals; it does not reform them.

But
● Figures suggest the new system works better.
● Offenders have to realise they have hurt someone and accept that what they have done is wrong.
● Some victims are helped to get over the effects of crimes.
● Young people's lives can be changed.

For **Task c)** you might include these points:
● Some victims (for example, elderly people) might be scared to meet young offenders.
● Some youngsters might just say the right thing but not really mean it.
● It is complicated to organise and needs a lots of preparation on both sides.
● The mediator needs to be well trained to handle things carefully.

Other relevant points would get you marks if you back the ideas up and develop them.

REMEMBER: 4 marks = 4 points = about 4 minutes spent.

Task 3

Mark your answers. If you missed any of the points, check back and see where they came from. Ensure that if you were asked the questions again you would get them right.

Mark ➡ Check ➡ Test

Extension work: Blending note-taking, comprehension and analysis.

Read the account below and answer the questions that follow:

The Wild West?

Large numbers of the houses are empty and vandalised. What kind of disaster has happened here? 'These are handsome, postwar, semi-detached houses with gardens … [but] … few people want to live here'. Brian Mumby, chairman of the Halton Moor Estate Management Board tells a familiar story. 'When I moved to this estate it was great. The kids even obeyed the "Keep off the Grass" signs.'

Community resources

We are talking in the estate's [new] One Stop and Community Centre, where you can pay your rent, ask about your benefits, see your probation officer or social worker, and consult your local councillor. It is one room shared by a pensioners' group, mothers and toddlers, and the Youth Forum, whose main activity is running bingo sessions for the pensioners. Brian confirms that most of the problems on the estate are caused by youths, and then tells me the youth club is only open 2 hours a week. He is aware of the irony.

Failed initiatives

Halton Moor was given £23 million urban renewal money by a Conservative Government in 1992. It has been spent on renovations, fortifications and anti-joyriding measures. Already the renovations are being renovated. The joyriders see the concrete barriers and bollards as a challenge. Boy racers have turned joyriding into a synchronised sport … After grass-churning victory runs they jump from the cars and set fire to them before running to a safe house.

continued …

Shops and leisure facilities?

There is a row of village-style shops overlooking the green. Only one, the newsagent, is open. The rest are burned out and boarded up. Brian wants to demolish this eyesore and build a community centre here. Leeds City Council has offered him £150,000. Brian scoffs: 'That's a living room and a kitchen.' He needs a million-and-a-half and plans to go to the EU and the Lottery for the money … The next day there are three burned-out cars on the green. Malcolm, a gloomy youth of few words, rides up on his bike. He looks into the gaping bonnets of the cars with almost professional interest. I ask why joyriding is so popular here. 'It's a crap estate.' I ask if things have improved since a Labour Government was elected. 'No, if owt, it's got crapper.'

Politicians and the poor

It suits the main political parties to talk about voter apathy. They like to give the impression that the electorate is too idle to vote [but] the Halton Moor estate electorate is as lively and intelligent as any group of people I've come across. The withdrawal of their vote is a statement of their contempt for politicians. The very poor are getting poorer, and nobody seems to care.

[Based on article by Sue Townsend in the *Observer*, 20 May 2001]

a) After reading the article on pp.21–22, **organise your notes in a spidergram** with the question 'What are the problems of deprived urban neighbourhoods?' in the middle.

b) There is little that politicians can do to help a community like this; the community should do more to help itself.' **Using the source and your own knowledge how far do you agree with this view?**

Task 5

Read these conclusions to question 2. Each conclusion is by a different student.

Extract 1 (Grade F)

The writer slags off politicians as timid and useless and I agree they can't do much to help – look how much money they've poured down the drain already on the useless road scheme. The community should do more to help itself. Young people should work harder at school and not vandalise things. People should go out and get some jobs.

Extract 2 (Grade C)

The writer describes the problems of poor estates, such as housing, crime, poor community facilities and the lack of hope of the people. From my own knowledge, I know that politicians can do some things to try to help so I don't totally agree with the quote – for example, local government can work to try to improve the environment and it might be possible to get money from other places like the Lottery or Europe. The community should do more to help itself – they might try neighbourhood watch schemes. They really need a Community Centre to get some pride back.

Extract 3 (Grade A)

The problem for the politicians is to rebuild a sense of community that isn't there. They can do things to help. Like the residents, the author is critical of politicians who don't seem to care but there are specific ways to tackle some of the problems. For example, the government has set up neighbourhood renewal action teams to bring together the work of local councils, businesses, schools, the police, and youth and social workers. The estates need money spending on them but why not consult local people about how the money is spent? They could be involved in plans for the Community Centre. The Courts also need to take a firm line with the regular trouble-makers, for example, antisocial behaviour orders.

It is hard for the community to help itself – lots of poverty, unemployment, a lack of hope, school truancy etc. – but not impossible: for example, there might be community projects in local schools. The council might appoint neighbourhood wardens to back up the police.

a) Why would Extract 2 be awarded a higher grade than Extract 1?

b) List the qualities of Extract 3 which you cannot find in the other two.

c) Look again at your answer to Question 2. How could you improve it?

Examiner's Summary

- Read widely on topical issues to develop your understanding and skills and practise on other texts.
- Expect to draw out key points and 'facts' from texts and to give your opinion.
- Unless you are asked to list information, try to *analyse* text, rather than just repeating what it says.
- Answer the question that has been set and notice how many marks are available.

Unit 5 Citizenship Issues in the News

Targets

1. To understand how Citizenship Studies relates to the 'news' agenda.
2. To be able to interpret and analyse news articles.
3. To understand the role of the media in society and the importance of a free press in providing information and affecting opinion.

Skill1: Understanding how Citizenship Studies relates to the media

The media – and newspapers in particular – plays quite an important part in your Citizenship Studies course. It is both a valuable source for your study of Citizenship themes and also a topic which you need to understand in its own right. When it comes to the examination you might be asked to show an understanding of:

FOCUS

Analysing the media

- How current social and political issues are reported in different news media.
- How the media can be used to promote particular causes.
- How effective different kinds of media are for different audiences.
- The significance and importance of the media in local, national, and international contexts.
- Issues relating to the freedom of the press, for example, individuals 'right to privacy' and the case for and against media censorship.

Task 1

a) **Look at one particular news story which interests you**. See how a range of different newspapers from a single day – including tabloids and broadsheets – cover the event. [For example, compare the websites of the *Sun* (www.thesun.co.uk) and the *Guardian* (www.guardian.co.uk).

b) **Then look at the coverage of the story in different media**, such as TV, radio, or the Internet. Pick out the main differences between the ways in which events are reported. Make a list of the ways in which these differences might be explained.

You have more skills than you might think when it comes to interpreting newspaper articles and other media stories. For example:

- You will have studied media texts in your English classes and considered the *purpose* of media texts and how *form*, *language*, *layout*, and *presentation* contribute to the effects of these texts.
- You will have thought about the *audience* or readership of texts and how people *select* and *respond* to texts such as newspaper articles.
- You will have analysed sources and interpretations in history lessons, including newspaper articles, and thought about issues such as *bias*, *reliability* and the *utility* of different sources of information.
- You may, in religious education (RE) or key stage 3 Citizenship/PSHE classes, have studied aspects of the significance of the media in society in relation to propaganda, stereotyping and promoting causes and campaigns. You may even be taking Media Studies as a separate GCSE.

REMEMBER! Be positive about some of the transferable skills that you already have in relation to analysing the media.

Task 2

Choose one of the following 'media texts':

- a front-page tabloid news story
- a broadcast of *Newsbeat* on Radio 1
- the BBC Internet news service (news.bbc.co.uk)
- a children's magazine-style weekend TV broadcast.

Write down answers to the following six questions:

1. What is the form of the report?
2. What is the content (what happens)?
3. What is the purpose (information, persuasion, entertainment)?
4. Who has produced this text?
5. What is the audience? (Has the story been 'tailored' to a particular audience?)
6. What meaning is conveyed and how? (What is the balance between fact and opinion? How objective is the story?)

Try to keep up with current news stories. It is good to read a broadsheet newspaper now and then to keep yourself up to date.

EXAMINER'S TIP!

Skill 2: Revising and defining key words

FOCUS
Key words

There are certain facts it will be helpful for you to know so that you can demonstrate your knowledge in an examination. For example:

- What are the different types of media?
- What evidence exists of the power of the media in influencing opinion?
- What laws limit what the media can and cannot do?

You will also need detailed knowledge (with examples) of the arguments for and against limits on the freedom of the press. Being able to define and then use key words and concepts in your answers will be a big advantage.

Key words – vocabulary palette

Censorship   Cheque-book journalism   Press Complaints Commission   Libel law
Right to privacy   Press 'baron'   Media intrusion   Official Secrets Act   Public interest
Freedom of information   Propaganda   Bias   Tabloid   Broadsheet   Paparazzi
Journalists   Gagging order   Editorials   Press responsibility   Local press
News agencies   Readership   Objectivity   Media 'spin'   Investigative journalism
Campaigning journalism   Freedom of expression

Task 3

Everyone has the right to freedom of opinion and expression; this right includes freedom to hold opinions without interference and to seek, receive and impart information and ideas through any media and regardless of frontiers.

[Article 19 of the United Nations' *Universal Declaration of Human Rights*, 1948]

a) **From the vocabulary palette above choose four words or phrases which support Article 19** of the UN declaration in relation to freedom of the media. Write two or three sentences which explain and define each of your choices.

Identify and know key words for understanding the media.

EXAMINER'S TIP!

b) **Now choose four words or phrases which would help you to argue that sometimes the press abuses its freedom** and that there should be some limits on its activities. Again, in a few sentences explain why you have chosen these words and what they mean.

Skill 3: Applying skills of media analysis to specific Citizenship examination requirements

The Citizenship Studies examination boards provide different opportunities for you to show your understanding of the role of the media in society. For two out of three of the boards, in one part of the paper you will be presented with a range of sources of information, which might include reports, speeches, textbook extract, graphs, statistics, photographs or cartoons, as well as newspaper reports. You might be asked a short-answer question about the report but are more likely to be asked to compare and contrast the newspaper account with the other sources.

Other ways in which you might be asked to use a newspaper source are:

● Demonstrate that you understand the main points in an article.
● Explain differences in the way that the same event is reported.
● Show how the press is important within local communities or can function as one element of a local campaign.

Task 4

Source A:

Press release
MOLTON PLC: WORLDWIDE RE-STRUCTURING ANNOUNCEMENT

Following the downturn in the US economy, Molton plc will be announcing world-wide job losses. Up to 14,000 employees could lose their jobs out of a total workforce of 40,000. We estimate that cost savings will help to return the company to profit within two years, maintain a dividend to shareholders and also reduce borrowing.

The company regrets to announce the closure of its UK factory at Pullbury in South Wales, with the loss of 1,200 jobs. We wish to do all in our power to support workforce at this difficult period and plan practical talks with Trade Union representatives, local politicians and regional economic agencies.

Source B:

Press release
MOLTON MELTDOWN: BODY BLOW TO PULLBURY

Local MP, Rees Jones has described the closure as devastating and a deathblow – 'Molton is the major employer in the area. We worked hard to get government and EU funding to persuade Molton to locate here in 1990 – this is a kick in the teeth.' Local business leaders blamed the strong pound and high labour costs in the UK for the company's decision. At the factory gate, foreman Bill Smith reported low morale among his colleagues: 'As a small, isolated, former mining community it's always going to be hard to get other companies to come here. Some of us may never work again.' Rees Jones has promised to work with the local council and business and union leaders to try to get the decision changed.'

Each relevant point
will usually = one
mark on short-answer
questions.

EXAMINER'S TIP!

a) **With reference to Sources A and B, why has Molton plc decided to close the Pullbury factory?** (*Five marks*)

b) **How can the differences in the tone and content of the two sources be explained?** (*Ten marks*)

[For answers see the end of this unit.]

You might also be asked a bigger question with a larger proportion of marks attached to it, such as 'Using the sources and your own knowledge, explain what action could be taken by the local community to stop the closure.' Here you would need to make reference to the role of the local and national media in any kind of campaign as one part of your answer.

Task 5

Using a newspaper source for your coursework

One of the examination boards asks you to write an 800 word account, comparing two sources of information of your choice, as a coursework item. One of these sources might be a newspaper article. You can practise the skill here.

Source A: The identity card debate

The last time people in the UK had to carry identity (ID) cards was during the Second World War. They were abolished in 1952. The terrorist acts which occurred in New York in September 2001 and the so-called 'invasion' of asylum seekers from continental Europe have led to calls to reintroduce ID cards. The UK is a relatively unpoliced society. In other European nations, citizens and refugees must carry ID cards and present them to the authorities if requested. Some politicians suggest that the fact that the UK does not insist on people carrying proof of identity is one reason why asylum seekers cross Europe to reach the UK.

Advances in technology mean that an ID card could now incorporate features that would be much harder to forge. It could, for example, include automatic fingerprint recognition or iris recognition (when the card is swiped it can 'see' the unique pattern of your iris).

In October 2001 an opinion poll showed that 86% of people were in favour of some form of ID card. It is argued that innocent people have nothing to fear and that it might help the police in tracing suspects, combatting credit-card fraud and other crimes involving stolen identities.

[Adapted from *GCSE Citizenship Studies*, Folens, 2001]

Source B: ID cards – a dumb idea and dangerous too

The appeal of compulsory ID cards is obvious – it sounds a simple way of controlling illegal immigrants, criminals and welfare fraudsters. Libertarian concerns that we should be presumed innocent and left to go free about our business without having to justify or identify ourselves seem remote.

On critical inspection, claims that 'Smart' ID cards will solve all our woes evaporate. The police explain that they almost never have problems identifying suspects, only in catching and convicting them. The immigration service explain that all illegal immigrants can, and most do, claim asylum, at which point their fingerprints are stored on a central computer and they are given an identity document without which they cannot legally obtain benefits or jobs.

There is every difference in the world between cards we carry voluntarily and being forced to carry one. If you forget your credit card it is an inconvenience. But if you step out of your home without your compulsory ID or forget to inform the government of a change of address you would commit a criminal offence. Even though the card would probably not help catch a single villain, it would criminalise many thousands of absent-minded, forgetful and inefficient people.

The idea of compulsory ID cards loses its appeal once people begin to think through the implications. When the government announced a scheme for ID cards in Australia, it received strong support in the polls but a massive 'No' campaign was launched. Concern focused on its implications for privacy. Eventually the polls showed nearly 90% against the proposal and it was dropped.

[Adapted from an article by Peter Lilley, former Conservative minister and Secretary for Social Security, 1992–97, the *Observer*, 30 June 2002]

In your assignment you will need to:

- Summarise the views expressed in each of the sources.
- Set the issue in context, by explaining the background to the events in question and relating it to the local, national or global picture.
- Identify and explain any bias that is evident in the sources.
- Express and justify your views on the matter in question, and suggest what you think might happen in the future.

Try this using Sources **A** and **B** on the issue of identity ID cards.

Extension Task

You may be asked an essay question on an issue relating to the media and society. There is more help and guidance on how to structure your extended writing in Units 8–9 of this book so you might want to look at these units before attempting the questions below. Also remind yourself of the key words in the vocabulary palette for this unit. Ask your teacher for feedback and advice if you attempt one of the questions below:

- 'There should be no limits on the freedom of the press.' Do you agree with this view? Give reasons for your opinion, showing that you have considered another point of view.
- 'Censorship is a price worth paying to protect a country's interests.' Discuss whether the media should be restricted in what they disclose.
- How influential and powerful do you think that the media is?

Answers to:

4a) US economic downturn, global company re-structuring, need to cut costs, strong pound, and high labour costs would all get credit. Additional development or explanation of any two of these would be likely to gain you full marks.

4b) Accounts have different purposes/audiences. Source A – tone = detached, justifying the action taken; context of global, rational economic decision; re-assuring primarily shareholders but also workforce. Source B – tone = emotive, more use of adjectives; emphasis on human effects of the decision and impact upon the town/community. More emphasis on politics than economics in B. It is natural for local newspaper to report community implications.

Examiner's Summary

- Identify and know key words for understanding the media.
- Practise analysing newspapers in terms of their content and opinions.
- Know the arguments for and against unlimited freedom of the press.

Unit 6 Using and Interpreting Statistics

FOCUS
Understanding statistics

Check the axes of graphs and the source of the information.

EXAMINER'S TIP!

Targets

1. To understand the different ways in which statistics can be presented.
2. To practice comprehension of statistics and analysis of statistical information for trends.
3. To appreciate the positive value and limitations of statistics.
4. To know how to use statistics for research and to support an argument.

Interpreting statistics is an important skill in the context of a GCSE Citizenship Studies examination paper and a potentially useful skill for your coursework. The Citizenship National Curriculum for 14–16-year-olds says that all young people should be able to show 'an awareness of the use and abuse of statistics'.

Skill 1: Analysing and drawing conclusions from statistics

Statistics can be presented in several ways, for example, as tables, block graphs, line graphs, or pie charts. These all allow for the presentation of numerical information. and are good for showing trends. When looking at graphs always check the two axes, in other words, what is written at the bottom and at the side – this will tell you what is being measured and how. Then look at the source of the information – consider whether it is authoritative and trustworthy.

Task 1, opposite, shows an example of drawing conclusions from statistics. You can then you can try a second example, Task 2, for yourself and check your answers at the end of the unit.

Task 1

Look at the graph on the opposite page and then answer the questions that follow.

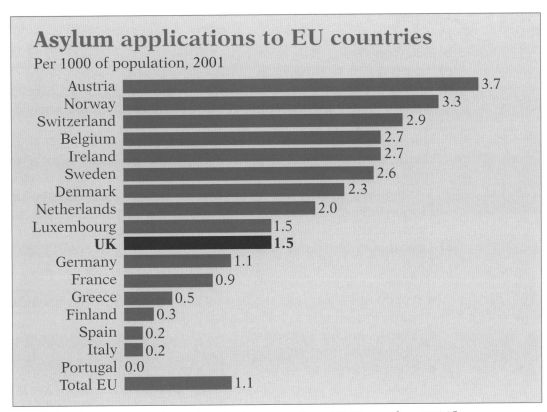

Asylum applications to EU countries

Per 1000 of population, 2001

Austria	3.7
Norway	3.3
Switzerland	2.9
Belgium	2.7
Ireland	2.7
Sweden	2.6
Denmark	2.3
Netherlands	2.0
Luxembourg	1.5
UK	**1.5**
Germany	1.1
France	0.9
Greece	0.5
Finland	0.3
Spain	0.2
Italy	0.2
Portugal	0.0
Total EU	1.1

['Call for sharing of refugee load', the *Guardian*, 28 December 2002]

FOCUS
Drawing conclusions from statistics

a) Which two European countries receive the highest number of asylum applications from refugees per 1,000 head of population? (*One mark*)

b) Name two countries which receive relatively few asylum applications. (*One mark*)

c) What is the average proportion of asylum applications across Europe? (*One mark*)

d) 'Britain takes more than its share of asylum seekers.' How far do the statistics support this view? (*Three marks*)

e) Using your own knowledge about the issue of asylum seekers, what do these figures not tell us? (What are the limitations of the statistics?) (*Five marks*)

Comprehension ➡ **Interpretation** ➡ **Wider context and knowledge**

Questions

The marks allocated to each question reflect their degree of difficulty.

a) – c) call for straightforward comprehension

d) calls for some interpretation of the statistics

e) asks you to put the sources in context and bring in some wider knowledge.

REMEMBER! Look at the mark allocation – spend more time on the questions which carry higher marks.

Answers

a) Austria and Norway.

b) Two from Spain, Italy or Portugal.

c) 1.1 per 1,000 of population

d) In support of the view, Britain receives more than the average number of applications of asylum applications per 1,000 of population (1.5 compared to 1.1). (*One mark*)

But against this, the UK actually lies below mid-table in 10th position in the EU for the number of asylum applicants per 1,000 head of population. (*One mark*)

The figures don't say how many asylum seekers each country 'takes', only proportionately how many applications are made – so the statement only receives partial support from the statistics. (*One mark*)

e) Lots of possible things to say which might gain you credit here – one mark for each developed point, for example:

- We do not know how the figures were collated by the UNHCR – were the same procedures followed in each country?
- Figures are for 2001 only – no sense of trends or information on differences from 2000 figures.
- Figures do not give total numbers of applicants but proportion per thousand head of population. They also do not indicate what proportion of applications for refugee status was accepted and what proportion had unfounded claims.
- Figures focus on Europe but in fact the developing world, not Europe, bears a much larger burden when it comes to offering shelter to refugees, including Iran, Pakistan and Tanzania.
- Figures do not indicate where the asylum seekers are coming from.
- Figures lack a human dimension – give no sense of the personal stories lying behind individuals' efforts to seek asylum in European countries.

To develop a point means you explain details and give examples, not just list ideas.

Task 2

Now look at the following table regarding the turnout in national elections. Think about the questions which follow.

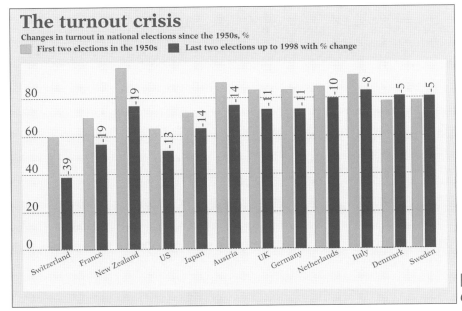

The turnout crisis

Changes in turnout in national elections since the 1950s, %

First two elections in the 1950s   Last two elections up to 1998 with % change

['Stay-at-home citizens', the *Guardian*, 1 May 2002]

a) What is the main conclusion that you can draw about trends in turnout at elections between the 1950s and 1998? (*Two marks*)

b) Which countries represent an exception to the main trend? (*One mark*)

c) The figures are generous to Britain. There was a big drop in the turnout for the 2001 General Election, to 59%. How would this affect the figure of –11 on the graph if you were to revise the UK % change from the 1950s? (*Two marks*)

d) Why should we care about what these statistics show? (*Five marks*)

e) Using your own knowledge, how might more people be encouraged to vote at local, national and European elections in Britain? (*Fifteen marks*)

Now check your answers at the end of the unit.

| Task 3 |

Look at the table on household waste and answer question a) on the following page.

Household waste recycled %
1998 unless stated

Switzerland	52
Germany	46
Netherlands	45
(1996) Austria	45
Sweden	35
Norway	34
(1997) Finland	30
Denmark	28
UK	12

['A family and its rubbish – an everyday story of unnecessary waste', the *Guardian*, 28 December 2002]

a) Put a ring around the statement below (1, 2, 3, or 4) that is a conclusion that *cannot* be drawn from the figures provided on re-cycling in the table on p.33:

1. Many European countries re-cycle more than a third of their household waste.
2. Britain has one of the worst records for re-cycling in Europe.
3. Much more domestic waste is produced in countries like Germany and Sweden.
4. Switzerland is a world leader in re-cycling.

Skill 2: Identifying the value and limitations of statistics

There are plenty of witty things that have been said criticising the value of statistics: for example Mark Twain (the nineteenth-century American novelist) famously said that there are 'lies, damned lies, and statistics'. It has also been said that 'Statistics should be used like a drunk man uses a lamp-post – for support not illumination.'

REMEMBER! Statistics are certainly open to interpretation. One person will argue that a glass is half-full, another that it is half empty, but they are both right.

Positive value of statistics

- Citizens need to be able to analyse public policy on the basis of rational evidence and some hard facts. It helps to have a clear, independent and fair measure of what is happening in different areas of public life. Statistical evidence, which should be given the same critical scrutiny as any kind of evidence, helps to provide some of the foundation stones of argument and debate.
- Statistics are important in the making of government policy but also in enabling voters to make a judgement as to whether government policies are working. The Office of National Statistics aims to provide a 'trusted source of the accurate and up-to-date knowledge we all need for the advancement of the government, business and people in the United Kingdom'.
- The statistical data from censuses every 10 years in the UK allows, for example, for the future planning of transport, schools, houses and facilities, locally and nationally.

Limitations of statistics

- The value of statistics depends upon the consistency and accuracy of the ways in which information is gathered and the questions that are asked
- They can be fabricated by unscrupulous political regimes (for example, Stalin and the 5-Year Plans for the Soviet economy in the 1930s) or 'spun' in democratic regimes.
- They can be partial and/or selective – measuring some things but not others.
- Some things, for example, human experiences, are very difficult to measure. Statistics can be rather dry and lacking a human dimension.
- The value of statistics can depend on the reliability of whoever is producing the information.
- They may represent a 'snapshot' and not show trends to indicate whether things are getting better or worse.

FOCUS
Value and limitations of statistics.

Task 4

a) What did Mark Twain mean when he talked about 'lies, damned lies, and statistics'? What would be the problems for a society where there were no statistics that anyone could trust?

b) How much 'truth' do statistics provide?

Skill 3: Using statistics to support an argument

Sometimes statistics are so powerful in the evidence that they provide that, collectively, they make an eloquent case for change.

Source A:

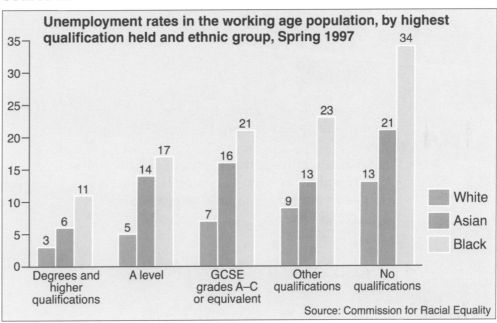

Unemployment rates in the working age population, by highest qualification held and ethnic group, Spring 1997

Source: Commission for Racial Equality

[P. Brett *et al.*, 2002, *Citizenship Studies at GCSE*, Folens, p.17]

Source B

The following statistics are taken from an article in the *Observer*, 29 December 2002, reporting on an independent study by a university professor examining data on 3,000 prisoners:

● Black people are six times more likely to be sent to prison than whites.
● Almost 25% of Britain's jail population (72,416) come from a minority ethnic background (ethnic minorities make up approx. 8% of the British population overall).
● If 'black Britain' were a separate country it would have the highest imprisonment rate in the world.
● Black people are five times more likely than white people to be stopped and searched by the police.
● Once arrested black British citizens are more likely to be remanded in custody than other offenders charged with similar offences and are more likely to receive a prison sentence for a first offence.

FOCUS
Statistics and argument

It was statistics like these (p.35, Sources A and B) that led Sir William MacPherson to define 'institutional racism' following his 1999 report into the police investigation of the murder of the black teenager Stephen Lawrence:

Institutional racism is:

the collective failure of an organisation to provide an appropriate and professional service to people because of their colour, culture, or ethnic origin. It can be seen or detected in processes, attitudes and behaviour which amount to discrimination through unwitting prejudice, ignorance, thoughtlessness and racist stereotyping which disadvantage minority ethnic groups.

[MacPherson Report]

Task 5

Consult the relevant sections on racial discrimination, inequality and the criminal justice system in your Citizenship textbooks and class notes.

a) **Draw at least three conclusions from Source A.** (*Three marks*)
b) **Explain at least two limitations of Source A.** (*Four marks*)
c) **In your opinion, how might the statistics in Source B be explained?** (*Eight marks*)

Skill 4: Using statistics in your research

FOCUS
Statistics and research

On your GCSE Citizenship Studies course you can expect to be both a user of data (finding out about different topic areas and identifying statistics to support your arguments) and a producer of data.

It is likely that you will use statistics to provide a context for your coursework project and include some in your appendices. Local and national government and the public services regularly issue statistics seeking to measure how and whether progress is being made in particular policy areas. Pressure groups also produce statistics to back up their arguments. The Internet is a good source for statistics (but make sure that you fully explain where you got your figures from).

You may create statistics of your own – through questionnaires, surveys and market research. The key thing here is for your evidence base to be as large and as representative as possible. You also need to think carefully about the questions you are asking. The value of a questionnaire will only be as effective as the questions that you choose to ask.

> If you include any statistics in your coursework project remember to make some effort to comment upon and analyse them in your main report.
>
> **EXAMINER'S TIP!**

Answers

Task 2

a) There has been a significant drop in turnout at national elections in the majority of advanced industrial democratic countries.

b) Denmark and Sweden.

c) The 1950s figure was 81% so the revised figure after the 2001 election in Britain would be –22.

d) Various possible answers would get you credit here, for example:

- General alienation and switch-off from politics and the political system indicates public dissatisfaction – worrying for democracy.
- Maybe shows government is becoming remote and disconnected from citizens – people feel excluded from democratic participation.
- Indicates that people don't trust politicians – associate them with sleaze and corruption.
- May allow the rise of extreme parties, such as that of the communists and fascists in the early twentieth century when democracy was discredited in some countries (or the British National Party [BNP] in the UK).
- There might be positive lessons to learn from Denmark and Sweden – why are these countries not experiencing the decline in participation?

e) This is a big Citizenship topic – too many answers to list here. Check your Citizenship textbooks and notes to see what points you might have left out!

Task 3: Statement 3 was a false conclusion.

Task 5:

a) All ethnic groupings stand a better chance of getting a job if they get a degree; whatever the level of qualification gained, unemployment rates are always higher among black people than their Asian or white colleagues; whatever the level of education, black people are generally around three times as likely to be unemployed as white counterparts.

b) Rather broad categories, for example, 'Asian' incorporates a large number of ethnic groups with big differences, for example between Chinese and Bangladeshis; 'black' incorporates those from African or Caribbean backgrounds. There is no gender breakdown to show the relative success of men and women from different ethnic groups.

c) Again, there are many possible answers to this question. Check your response against your textbook and notes on the Criminal Justice System, racism and discrimination. Ask a teacher, parent or friend what they think.

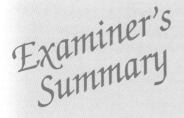

Examiner's Summary

- Check the axes of graphs and the source of statistical information.
- Practise drawing conclusions from different kinds of graphs.
- Know the value and limitations of statistics.

Unit 7 *Citizenship in Action: How to Plan, Research and Evaluate it*

Targets

1. To understand how to plan and structure your Citizenship coursework project.
2. To know some ways of finding things out and researching background information.
3. To be aware of some effective strategies for 'writing up' your Citizenship activity.
4. To understand how to evaluate your Citizenship coursework activity.

Probably the most important decision you will make is choosing your project. Choose one that you really want to do. Talk about this with your teacher and check how it relates to the Citizenship Studies course you are doing.

Your coursework will be based upon a Citizenship activity that involves working with other people in either a school or community setting. The opportunities for Citizenship projects are exciting. There are too many to list them all. The following are just a few of the possibilities:

- Undertaking a Citizenship project/investigation during your work experience.
- Involvement in a local or voluntary group aiming to bring about change (for example, related to an environmental issue).
- Organising a school or community-based charity activity/event.
- Organising a charity fund-raising activity as part of a national event (for example, Red Nose Day, Children in Need).
- Participation in a Citizenship activity in the wider world (for example, a foreign exchange visit or clean water campaign).

Remember: Coursework makes up 40% of your marks in Citizenship Studies and about a quarter of your marks in the examination paper will also allow you to write about your involvement in a Citizenship activity, thus it is important that you know what examiners are looking for in order to gain maximum credit for what you know, understand and can do.

Skill 1: How to plan your Citizenship activity

A successful plan for your Citizenship activity requires:

- a clear sense of purpose
- an explanation of what makes the project a Citizenship activity
- an outline of what research you will need to carry out

- a clear division of roles and responsibilities
- an action plan with time scales and staging posts
- reflection on the processes of planning, for example, consideration of different alternatives.

Task 1

1 **Identify**, clearly and explicitly, the aims, purpose and nature of the Citizenship activity and the scope for your participation.

2 **Brainstorm** the main idea. What makes this a Citizenship activity? If you are working with a group of other students plan who will do what. Does the activity have a value to other people? Identify possible problems with your project.

3 **Plan what research you will need to do.** What information do you need to find out and where will you find it?

4 **Create an action plan.** Break the activity down into smaller parts and specific tasks. List the intended outcomes. Explain your time scales and staging posts.

5 **Write up your plan.** Include what alternatives were considered and why they might have been rejected. Talk about advantages and disadvantages.

Five-stage planning

Keep all of your rough notes and a diary of what you do or plan to do.

EXAMINER'S TIP!

How to brainstorm

Tracey decided that the Citizenship focus of her work experience at the local supermarket would be to investigate the issue of Fair Trade coffee, which she had been learning about in the classroom. What was the supermarket's policy on Fair Trade products and what were the customers' attitudes towards Fair Trade goods?

Her brainstorming plan looked like this:

Revise class notes on Fair Trade issues.

Read supermarket's policy on Fair Trade issues.

Find out where supermarket's Fair Trade coffee comes from and the costs.

Research coffee production in country of origin.

Find out proportions of different coffee brands sold in the supermarkets.

FAIR TRADE COFFEE

Questionnaire for customers.

Presentation at end of the work experience.

Look at relevant websites.

Find out what it would take for people to change their shopping habits.

Analyse Fair Trade campaigns.

Talk with supermarket manager and/or person in charge of coffee section.

BIG QUESTIONS

How can people act locally to improve the quality of life for others globally?

What is the power of the 'active' citizen in the global economy?

Task 1

Plan your activity. With a group of three friends you agree that you want to raise funds for charities working with children in Africa. You decide to organise a quiz for Y7 pupils and their parents in about three months time. Brainstorm how you would plan this in order to make it a focused and successful Citizenship activity. Use the plan above for ideas. (**Clue:** think about what you need to research and who does what within your group.)

Skill 2: How to research your Citizenship activity

Your Citizenship coursework activity will partly be assessed on:

● The knowledge and understanding that you demonstrate of a Citizenship issue which underpins your activity.
● How well you obtain and explain the information that you collect.

In other words it is important that you carry out plenty of relevant background research.

You will need to gather and summarise a wide range of information and present it effectively in your written report. You also need to give your opinions and draw conclusions based on your research.

All the resources that you have used should be noted on a resources list and attached to your coursework report.

> **REMEMBER!** The key is how you *use* and *reflect upon* the data you have collected.

You will find that you will need to research your project from a wide variety of sources. These might include:

Official reports (for example, from Parliament, Local Government, voluntary organisations or pressure groups)

Textbooks/websites

Questionnaires/surveys that you have designed

Newspaper extracts

Interview notes/observational notes

Letters you have written and correspondence with organisations

Photographs/charts/diagrams/graphs/tables/statistics

Promotional literature

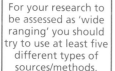

For your research to be assessed as 'wide ranging' you should try to use at least five different types of sources/methods.

EXAMINER'S TIP!

Task 2

a) **You see a TV news report about the poor working conditions of the people who make trainers.** These include long working hours and the use of dangerous chemicals and manufacturing equipment. A group of you decide that you want to do something to help and to join a campaign to persuade a multi-national company to introduce an ethical code of conduct for its workers. How might you find out more about this issue?

b) **Who might you contact in order to make sure of your facts?**
(**Clue:** *find out more about the role of Development Education Centres and the Local Agenda 21 Project.*)

c) **What might you do with the information once you have done your research?**

Skill 3: Writing up the activity

FOCUS

Demonstrating knowledge and understanding

When writing up the Citizenship activity you need to show how much knowledge and understanding you have gained from the activity itself and from researching the wider issues. Your report will get higher marks if it is analytical rather than descriptive. If the project is based around a key question it is more likely to help you to produce sustained explanation rather than simply describe what you did.

Task 3

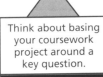

Think about basing your coursework project around a key question.

EXAMINER'S TIP!

This is a section from a report by Paul which would receive a top grade:

For my project I organised (with the help of eight friends, my parents and teachers) a bring and buy sale for the Blue Peter Waterworks' appeal. The aim was to help groups of people in Tanzania install purifying pumps and also to provide improved education to build pumps in the future so the people become self-dependent. The project also aimed to raise awareness of citizenship issues throughout the school, such as the plight of people in Africa. Often in Tanzania, particularly at times of drought, people cannot rely on getting clean water from day to day and have to walk several miles to collect and carry water by hand (see www.wateraid.co.uk).

I decided to write to companies and also produce notices for people in school asking them to donate goods to be sold at the sale. I put posters around the school, notices in registers and put an advertisement in the school newsletter to inform people of the event. I created a questionnaire and quiz for Year 10 students based upon information in the Blue Peter pack (which also included posters and price labels). I visited the site management team to outline my plan, book the hall and some large tables. On the day of the sale my friends and I took the preceding lesson off to set up the tables, organise the products and put up more posters and information. We also sold some raffle tickets in the staffroom. It was well supported by staff and students. We raised just over £100 in an hour.

continued ...

Tanzania Waterworks Appeal

Bring & Buy Sale

**School Hall
3 October
3.30pm**

I was proud to have played a pivotal role in the organising, setting up and running of this bring and buy sale. I also had excellent help from my friends, family teachers and peers. The experience was an eye opener as to what some peoples' lives are like in the developing world. It made me appreciate that campaigns like the Blue Peter appeal really can help. I am privileged to live in a developed country with a secure economy which provides advantages like not only clean water, but clean running water on tap.

I might have improved the project by holding it on a date which didn't coincide with Comic Relief fundraising, as this prevented some people from attending the sale. Details of this project could be listed in the school library or on the school website, making it easier for others to access the contacts and ideas used. It could be an annual event to raise money for other charities, local, national or international.

[Adapted from a real coursework project undertaken in 2003 – Congratulations to the student concerned!]

a) Write down the effective examples of:
- planning
- citizenship knowledge and understanding
- organisation of the activity
- opinion/reflection/self-evaluation.

b) What are the obstacles that make this kind of activity difficult?

c) Why do you think that Paul's project was so successful?

GCSE COURSEWORK: WRITING UP THE CITIZENSHIP ACTIVITY
- Indicate how and why you became involved.
- Say what you and others actually did – including your duties and responsibilities.
- Show what research you did and why.
- Provide some contextual knowledge linking your project to the Citizenship curriculum. (Some of this research could be presented in the form of appendices – consult your teacher for advice on this.)
- Note whether information was easy/difficult to obtain and what was useful.
- Don't undersell yourself – if you were fully involved in the activity, say so.
- Give your opinions and draw conclusions from what you have learned.
- Get people to read your first draft – friends, parents, etc. – ask them for comments and then re-draft.

> **REMEMBER:** The word limit is 1,500–2,000 words (check the precise limit with your teacher). You may need to re-draft and use an appendix if your report is too long.

FOCUS
Evaluation

Skill 4: Evaluating your coursework project

The evaluation stage comes last but it is still very important. The key is to evaluate what you did, what others did, what was achieved, what lessons you learned and what could have been improved.

You will need to draw together your opinions and conclusions, clearly stating:

- Your role, views, experience and contribution to the activity.
- Your active involvement over a period of time (the more active the better).
- The good and bad points of the project, your Action Plan and the strategies used.
- What you learned and what you and others gained from undertaking the activity.
- Your opinions/reflections/conclusions on the activity and its value to others.
- What changes you would recommend that might have improved the activity.

Task 4

Organising a Youth Football Tournament in Fitzrovia

Trouble between young people and residents/racial tension
The Warren playground is in a part of London called Fitzrovia. For years it was run-down and vandalised. Local residents were worried by behaviour around the site and got up a petition about it. Teenagers and young adults mainly of Asian origin (Bengali), would park their cars, play loud music, drink and maybe smoke cannabis. There was broken glass and litter everywhere. There was racial tension in the area between white and Asian youths.

The big dream
Then a group of young people had the idea of holding a five-a-side football tournament on it. André, one of the young men involved, tells the story: 'There was massive interest. So we started meeting in the playground on Sunday afternoons to plan it – there were about ten of us. The big dream was to raise £500 and get 16 teams from the local community.'

Encountering opposition
'[But] the local residents were dead against it. They said the playground was for children not teenagers. The police were also concerned. Then we got told that the football pitch actually belonged to the parks department. They were just as suspicious as everyone else to begin with. Worst of all, they were going to charge us £100 for the use of the pitch -- and we had no money.'

continued …

A different slant

We had a meeting and agreed that to get people on our side we would need to put a different slant on the tournament. So we decided to make it a tournament against vandalism. We would clean up all the rubbish in the playground. Then with any money raised from the tournament we'd do something to improve the area. We had to convince the people who used to hang out at the playground not to come to drink, or smoke drugs or play their music late at night.'

Building support

'We opened a bank account, put in a small amount of our own money and started to look to local businesses. We produced a leaflet and were lucky when the boss of a local design firm ran off 500 copies for us. By now we'd cleaned up the playground. What a difference! Word began to get round. So we went back to the residents. We knocked on every door, and told people we wanted to do this tournament to help clean up the area.

We organised a petition and got people to sign it. We printed out a list of all the local businesses who were supporting us and the young people who had pledged to steward the event on the day. It was obvious we had massive community support. Finally the support of Camden Council made us official.'

The day of the tournament

'Everyone had said we couldn't organise a tournament on such a small pitch, but we worked out a schedule of teams to play. Instead of having all 16 at once, we had 8 in the morning and 8 in the afternoon, and then the final! We invited the mayor and the councillors. The boys brought their own sound system, blasting out rap and hip-hop. We also put up a display of us clearing up the playground. It showed everyone what we had done.'

[Abridged and adapted from Ted Huddleston, *Changing Places* (The National Youth Agency and the Citizenship Foundation, 2002)]

Keep a copy of your Citizenship coursework report and re-read it in the week before your examination in order to refresh your memory of your involvement and the planning and evaluation undertaken.

EXAMINER'S TIP!

a) What do you think André learned as a result of his involvement in this project?

b) What was the value of the project to the community?

c) This was an excellent project but can you think of any ways in which it might have been improved?

When you come to do your GCSE Citizenship Studies coursework it may not be as ambitious as some of the activities outlined in this Unit. You will need to be realistic. You will probably have a limited amount of time to complete the coursework and it is important that what you choose to do is achievable. Nevertheless, this Unit should have given you some ideas for producing a good coursework report.

Examiner's Summary

- Make sure that you are clear about in what way your project is a Citizenship activity.
- Have a clear plan of action.
- Build wide-ranging research and contextual knowledge into your report.
- Give opinions about what you and others have learned.
- Sum up the project's strengths and how it could have been improved.

Unit 8 Structuring your Extended Writing on Citizenship Themes

Targets

1. To improve planning for extended writing by:
- selecting and sorting relevant material for an answer
- structuring a response
- improving the way in which ideas link together.

Skill 1: Realising why extended writing is hard

Extended writing is difficult because you have to do so many things at once. You have to:

- **Remember what you want to say and select the right material to keep your answer relevant to the question.**
- **Sort your ideas into a structure which give them meaning.** This is difficult where abstract concepts such as democracy, freedom, and rights are being used.
- **Distinguish between the general and the particular,** balancing your 'big points' – often the first sentence of a paragraph – with your 'particular' material, for example, details and examples that support the big points.
- **Know the right words to link your ideas together.**

This Unit is designed to help you to build up your skills in extended writing. You will be required to write an essay in your Citizenship Studies examination which will count for between a quarter and a third of your examination mark. You will probably find this the hardest part of the exam.

In this Unit we will now build up an answer to the following sample examination question. You should be able to apply the techniques used to planning any Citizen Studies question.

Why is the Human Rights Act (HRA) important for protecting the rights of UK citizens?

FOCUS *Creating a framework for your ideas*

Task 1

Find all your textbooks and class notes on this topic so that you have them to hand to help to flesh out a writing frame for this topic. **Make some 'spider-gram' notes on the Human Rights Act** (HRA) (see Unit 4 for guidance on note-taking).

Skill 2: Creating a writing frame

When revising, you will need to develop your ability to plan essays quickly and effectively. When you were younger your teachers may have given you writing frames – in other words paragraph headings which helped to give your essays a skeleton framework. Organising your own writing frames for different topics at GCSE level can help you to sort your thinking.

Task 2

This task is designed to help you to 'theme' information under more general headings and develop relationships between big points and supporting 'little' points.
Photocopy this and the following page, cut up the sixteen points (A–P) and sort them into whatever pattern you like. You may add extra information slips from your own notes.

A Historically, the rights of UK citizens have not been well defined. For a long time, Parliament was reluctant to make the European Convention on Human Rights part of UK law because it would interfere with Parliament's right to decide law.

B Since 2000, new laws made by the UK Parliament must, as far as possible, follow the terms of the HRA.

C The model Naomi Campbell used the HRA to try to protect her privacy when a national newspaper pictured her attending a Narcotics Anonymous meeting.

D In May 2001, some protesters at an anti-capitalist rally in London complained that they were being denied their right to peaceful protest – public safety and protection of property were given priority.

E The UK Parliament can overrule the HRA in the event of war or in the interests of preventing terrorism, and on the grounds of national security.

F Taking cases to the European Court of Justice is a long, difficult and expensive process.

G In 2001 a court found that the two boys who committed the murder of James Bulger in 1993, when they were 10 – Jon Venables and Robert Thompson – had the right under the HRA to have their whereabouts protected from publication by the press. The court concluded that they would face the risk of death or serious injury if their addresses were revealed. Here 'freedom of expression' competed with the 'right to life'.

H During the 30 years prior to 2000, the UK government was judged to have broken the European Convention on Human Rights over 50 times.

I Important Articles of the HRA provide for fundamental rights (for example, the right to life and the right not to be subjected to torture), procedural rights (for example, the right to a fair trial), and qualified rights (such as freedom of expression and the right to privacy).

J The HRA provides stronger protection for equal opportunities: it states that everyone should have the right not to be treated differently because of their race, religion, gender or any other status.

K Some rights under the HRA, such as freedom of expression, are 'qualified' and may be restricted by the UK Parliament, for example, for public safety or to protect the rights of others.

L Diane Pretty, who suffered from the wasting Motor Neurone Disease, lost her case under the HRA in April 2002 seeking to protect her husband from prosecution if he helped her to die. It was rules that this would conflict with Article 1 in the European Convention on the right to life.

M The HRA is enormously important for protecting the rights of UK citizens because it incorporates a whole series of fundamental human rights historically recognised by the UN (1948) and the European Convention on Human Rights (1950) as legal rights law. Now, if someone believes their rights have been abused, they can apply directly to the British courts.

N It is important to recognise that different UK citizens will want to 'protect' different rights. Moreover, sometimes rights will conflict – the HRA still has to be tested in many areas.

O The HRA draws upon ideas in the UN Universal Declaration of Human Rights, including protection from unfair arrest, the right to an education, and freedom of assembly.

P In the 1970s and 1980s parents went to court to oppose caning of their children. They lost in the UK but won in Europe. It was a long time before caning was banned in UK schools. In a similar case today, courts in the UK could decide, using the new HRA.

FOCUS *Identifying big points and supporting details*

Task 3

Now think about the relationship between the points labelled with the letters. M A I N and the rest. **Arrange the points into an essay plan and use the M A I N points to help with the first sentence of each paragraph**.

You could simply arrange the points and choose from the menu of connecting statements to help to link them up. Hopefully, you will choose to be more ambitious than this and use the ideas as a starting point and framework only. You should try to include ideas from your notes generated in Task 1.

M	**A**	**I**	**N**
The HRA is enormously important for protecting the rights of UK citizens because it incorporates a whole series of fundamental human rights historically recognised by the UN (1948) and the European Convention on Human Rights (1950) into legal rights law, so now courts of law can protect people in the UK (and Europe).	Historically, the rights of UK citizens have not been so well defined or protected. For a long time, Parliament was reluctant to make the European Convention on Human Rights part of UK law because it would interfere with Parliament's right to decide law.	Important Articles of the HRA provide for fundamental rights (for example, the right to life and the right not to be subjected to torture), procedural rights (for example, the right to a fair trial), and qualified rights (such as freedom of expression and the right to privacy).	It is important to recognise that different UK citizens will want to protect different rights. Moreover, sometimes rights will conflict – the HRA still has to be tested in many areas.
F Taking cases to the European Court of Justice could be a long, difficult and expensive process. **J** The HRA provides stronger protection for equal opportunities. **P** In the 1970s and 1980s parents went to court to oppose caning of their children. They lost in the UK but won in Europe. It was a long time before caning was banned in UK schools. In a similar case today, courts in the UK could decide, using the new HRA.	**H** During the 30 years prior to 2000, the UK government was judged to have broken the European Convention on Human Rights over 50 times. **E** The UK Parliament can overrule the HRA in the event of war, to prevent terrorism, or on the grounds of national security. **B** Now new laws made by the UK Parliament must, as far as possible, follow the terms of the HRA.	**O** The HRA draws upon ideas in the UN Universal Declaration of Human Rights including … . **L** Diane Pretty case … . **K** Some rights under the HRA are 'qualified' and may be restricted by Parliament (for example, Freedom of expression,) for public safety, or to protect the rights of others. (for example, freedom to hold raves; freedom for BNP to march in some areas).	**G** Bulger case … . **D** In May 2001, some protesters at an anti-capitalist rally in London complained that they were being denied their right to peaceful protest – public safety and protection of property were given priority. **C** Naomi Campbell privacy case against a national newspaper … .

Skill 3: Connecting your ideas together

If you do not have a good supply of connecting words (connectives) and good ways of beginning sentences and paragraphs, it will make it harder for you to demonstrate your ability to evaluate, interpret or explain and you are less likely to gain higher marks. On the other hand, you are more likely to gain higher marks if you can use connectives because it will give your work more fluency. These kinds of words and phrases help you to show the relationship between one fact and another.

Task 4

Practise using each of the connectives shown below to link two of the labelled statements, A–P, or material from your own notes on human rights.

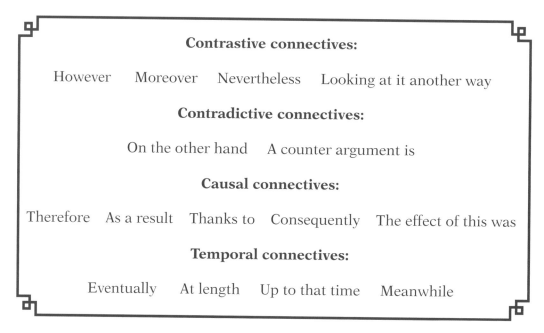

Contrastive connectives:

However   Moreover   Nevertheless   Looking at it another way

Contradictive connectives:

On the other hand   A counter argument is

Causal connectives:

Therefore   As a result   Thanks to   Consequently   The effect of this was

Temporal connectives:

Eventually   At length   Up to that time   Meanwhile

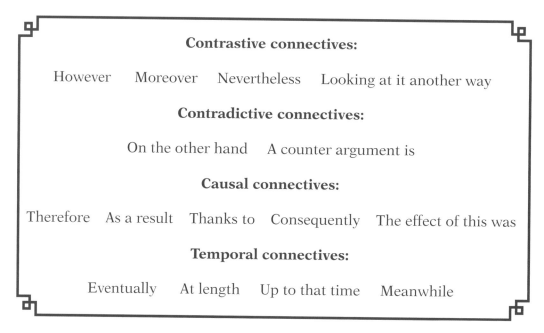

Using a range of different linking words and phrases increases the fluency of your writing.

EXAMINER'S TIP!

Skill 4: Answering the question, introductions, and conclusions

It is worth reminding yourself again of the title of the question (and should keep doing so while you are writing your essay in the examination):

Why is the Human Rights Act important for protecting the rights of UK citizens?
You could include the following in your answer, along with information of your own:

● There are legally recognised basic rights.
● How the Human Rights Act is used in UK and European courts.
● The role of Parliament in relation to the rights of UK citizens.
● Relevant recent court cases.

In the examination it is not compulsory for you to follow the suggested structure and bullet points given, in brackets, after each examination question. You will not be penalised for developing your own approach to the question. HOWEVER, the guidance is there for a reason – if you ignore the bullet points, there is a danger that you will fail to answer the question directly and may include irrelevant information that the examiners will find it hard to give you credit for.

EXAMINER'S TIP!

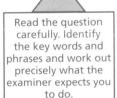

FOCUS *Answering the question in a direct and relevant way from start to finish*

Read the question carefully. Identify the key words and phrases and work out precisely what the examiner expects you to do.

EXAMINER'S TIP!

You should now have an idea, from Tasks 1–4, of how you are going to organise the content of this essay. There is obviously more than one way to do this and you might have identified some big points of your own or felt that some of the little points could be re-phrased and promoted to big points.

Now we need to think about:
● how you can stay focused on the question
● how you are going to start the essay
● how you might end the essay.

> **Focusing on the question:** It is a common complaint in GCSE Examiner's Reports that many candidates fail to address directly the question they have been asked.
> ◆ On 'why' questions, examiners are usually looking for candidates to rank factors in order of priority and decide which are the more important reasons. This is a useful task for you to carry out in order to clarify your thinking and start to organise paragraphs in order.
> ◆ Examiners also expect you to zone in on the key words of questions.
> ◆ Try to make sure that the first sentence of each paragraph directly addresses the question.

Task 5

Identify and underline the key words of the question.

> ## Introductions
>
> **DO:** Address the question directly right from the start.
>
> Identify the main issues and areas of debate raised by the question.
>
> Show that you understand the main point or points of a question.
>
> Use a telling fact or statistic which goes straight to the heart of the question, if you can remember a relevant one!
>
> **DON'T:** Plunge straight into description.
>
> Start to write everything you know about the subject.
>
> Waffle vaguely about events unrelated to the question.
>
> Start providing irrelevant background.

How long should an introduction be? A sentence is too little; a side of A4 too much – aim at about six to ten lines.

Conclusions

DO: Refer back to the question and answer it as clearly as you can.

Make sure that you reach a verdict and give your opinion.

Try to keep one telling detail in reserve, which supports your main points.

DON'T: Simply repeat what you have already said.

Throw in a new idea that you only thought of towards the end.

Task 6

Start to think about effective ways in which you might start and end this essay on human rights.

FOCUS

Writing accurately

Skill 5: Writing – putting it all together

Now you should be in a position to bring your answer together and write the essay. Most of the hard work has already been done. However, there are skills to emphasise at this point. Extra marks are awarded for 'quality of written communication'; for top marks from one of the examination boards you need to present: 'relevant information coherently, employing structure and style to render meaning clear. The text produced [must be] legible. Spelling, punctuation and grammar [must be] sufficiently accurate to render meaning clear.'

---

1. Spelling
- Many mistakes can be avoided; look particularly for doubling of letters; use of 'their', 'there', 'they're', etc. Also learn key Citizenship words and concepts (see Unit 3).

2. Expression
- Do not repeat yourself.
- Try to write formally, avoiding slang and abbreviation. Forget your normal text-messaging style.

3. Punctuation
- When you pause, consider using a full stop, comma or question mark.
- If you can use commas, colons and semi-colons properly, show the examiner.
- Do not forget apostrophes (for example, Greenpeace's tactics'; 'the media's right').
- Re-read your answer at the end and correct punctuation.

4. Paragraphing
- One-sentence paragraphs or long rambling ones usually suggest this is likely to be a weaker candidate.
- A variety of paragraph lengths suggests A*–C standard.
- Paragraphs that contain flowing sentences and link well come from the best candidates.

Write the first four or five paragraphs of your answer. Use your plan and keep re-reading the title.

Skill 6: Checking

Re-read the advice above and correct your response.
Count how many improvements you have made.

Skill 7: Knowing what the examiners are looking for

A good answer (in otehr words, Level 5: 21–25 marks out of 30) can be described as: 'A well-structured account that covers all of the main points in the question. The response has a clear structure and points are often supported by relevant examples. There is evidence of evaluative skills and a reasoned conclusion.' A Level 4 answer covers most of the main points, has a fairly clear structure and incorporates some examples. There is some evidence of evaluation and a conclusion. An excellent Level 6 account fully answers the question, has a clear, logical structure and well-chosen examples, and draws clear conclusions based on the question and the evidence provided.

Task 7

What level would you award yourself?

Nearer to the examination you will need to practise writing essays under timed examination conditions and without the material for the answers in front of you.

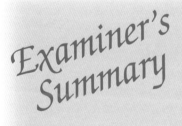
Examiner's Summary

- When revising, re-organise your notes on cards and try to identify big points and supporting examples.
- Read the question carefully and make sure that you try to answer it directly.
- In the examination take time to produce a detailed plan or writing frame: it is essential.
- Write carefully. Do not rush.

Unit 9 Writing to Argue

Skill 1: How to construct an argument

By the end of your GCSE Citizenship course you should be able to: 'express, justify and defend … in writing a personal opinion about [Citizenship] issues, problems or events' and 'be able to think about, express, explain and critically evaluate views that are not [your] own.'

To argue effectively you need to show that you are aware that there are different points of view. Do not just state what you believe; try to counter alternative points that have been made or could be made.

An argument is effective if it convinces the reader (in this case the examiner) or gives the reader cause to reconsider an opinion.

FOCUS
Argumentative writing

Writing to argue requires:
● a strong beginning and ending
● a logical structure
● details which can be used as proof
● an understanding of the alternative viewpoint
● logic which overcomes that other viewpoint.

Skill 2: Approaches to argumentative writing

The best thing to do when you need to express an argument is to plan carefully what you are intending to say before you begin to write. It is easy to get sidetracked, and careful planning will help you to avoid this.

You should aim to write a balanced argument; this means showing both points of view before drawing your conclusion and persuading your reader. One technique is to show the opposite point of view first and then show your reader why it does not work and that your way is better.

You can practise this approach in the example given opposite.
The basic organisation for an argumentative piece of writing is:

Opening	Middle	End
● make it clear to the examiner that you understand the question ● explain any terms and key words ● say what your point of view is. **Make it interesting.**	● explain your answer in detail ● make points in a logical sequence.	● sum up by re-stating your main argument. **Make it convincing.** ● make absolutely clear what you believe to be the main reasons, etc. – do not introduce any new information at this point.

Skill 3: The writing process

To be successful, you should follow a routine similar to that established in Unit 7 (p. 38):

1. **Identify** the significant words in question, the ones that tell you exactly what you must do. This will help you to focus on the question.

2. **Brainstorm ideas** – for example, produce a spidergram which contains your ideas about the subject.

3. **Organise ideas** into a list, so that they follow logically, and one point can be seen to lead naturally to the next. At this stage you can also decide what to put in your introduction and conclusion.

4. **Create a palette of extra details and key phrases** – some of these will be linking words which join ideas together (see Unit 8, p.46). If you complete all these stages before you begin to write, there should be no worries about you running out of ideas later.

5. **Write your answer and check your work**.

Read the following statement:

> **Pressure groups have too much power; they are dangerous for democracy.**

Do you agree with this view?
Give reasons for your opinion, showing that you have considered another point of view.

Stage 1

Identify the most important words. You could include the following points in your answer and other information of your own:

- What pressure groups are.
- Who they seek to influence and how.
- Different methods of protest.
- The role of pressure groups in a democracy.
- Case studies of pressure groups that you know about.

Stage 2

Brainstorm ideas for and against the statement (I have done this for you).

Brainstorm

Pressure groups too powerful/ dangerous for democracy

- Pressure groups sometimes break the law through their campaigns – use of violence = dangerous for democracy.
- They can influence local and national Government at the expense of the majority interest.
- Media stunts do not really explain issues.
- Undemocratic? A small group of people have the right to protest.
- Influence government leaders and so reduce the influence of backbench, elected MPs.
- Stop people joining political parties.
- Campaign on single issues so do not see the bigger picture.

Pressure groups a good thing/ important in a democracy

- Let governments know what people think.
- Represent powerless people without a voice, like the old or homeless.
- Represent issues which cross party lines, for example, capital punishment, abortion and countryside issues.
- They help people persuade governments.
- Sign of democracy that people have the right to protest.
- Provides information for the public. For example, in our local area … [fill in].
- Positive efforts of environmental pressure.
- A way for individuals to make a difference.

FOCUS

Beginnings and endings

Task 1

You decide to answer this question by first stating the argument against pressure groups, then putting more strongly the argument in favour of pressure groups.

Stages 3 and 4

Write down the points above in a logical order. If you can, add some extra details from your own knowledge.

Stage 5 Writing

Read this example of a possible opening to the essay:

In recent years, political parties have seen a fall in their membership, while pressure groups have seen a great increase in interest and membership. Does this mean that pressure groups have too much power now? In my opinion, pressure groups are not dangerous for democracy but an important part of democracy.

Task 2

Complete the above paragraph, then write the first sentence of the following paragraph, covering the first point you placed in your plan.

Now read this ending, which is equally firm:

Pressure groups are not too powerful – indeed they help to represent powerless people such as the homeless (Shelter) and the elderly (Help the Aged). They can also be an important democratic voice in local communities to campaign on particular issues of concern ...

Task 3

Add three more sentences to this ending, to sum up your argument and convince the reader that pressure groups play a valuable role in democratic countries.

> **Remember:** Interesting and convincing writing = Marks

Skill 5: Putting on the style

- Do not forget that vocabulary can have a big effect on the quality of your answer. Look back at the **connecting words** vocabulary palette in Unit 8.
- Try using some **emotive language** or persuasive techniques, like the word 'surely', to convince people to agree with you.
- A good technique is **second-guessing,** when you predict in advance what the objections might be and answer them.

Example: Although some might argue that pressure groups, such as Friends of the Earth, are bad for democracy because they focus narrowly on a single issue, this does not necessarily make them dangerous.

Use second-guessing when appropriate.

EXAMINER'S TIP!

Task 4

Write a sentence in which you mention the argument 'Media stunts by pressure groups do not explain issues' (to show that you know the issues), and then discredit the argument. Start with 'Although' or 'In spite of' or 'Even though'.

Include case studies and examples from your local area in your essays if you can.

EXAMINER'S TIP!

Extension Task

The final response

The following are the opening sentences for each paragraph of one response. Notice how the ideas seem to follow logically. They now need to be supported with evidence, examples, and details of pressure groups that you know about. Once you have read your notes through, you can begin to put some flesh on this skeleton answer. Bring in your knowledge of local events and campaigns – this will impress the examiner. As soon as you catch yourself wandering from the point – stop; re-read what you have done, and then go on without the extra unnecessary bits.

Paragraph 1

Pressure groups try to bring about change through bringing pressure to bear on politicians, businesses and the media. They vary in how much power they have …

Paragraph 2

The activities of pressure groups can be dangerous for democracy when they use violence or direct action to draw attention to their cause …

Paragraph 3
Some national pressure groups are powerful but not very representative of ordinary people – there are some dangers here ...

Paragraph 4
Overall, however, pressure groups play a valuable role in giving people an organised voice to campaign for changes on issues that they care about ...

Paragraph 5
In the area I live in there are several effective pressure groups I know about ...

Paragraph 6
Most pressure groups use peaceful and persuasive methods, which are completely democratic, to change people's minds ...

Paragraph 7
Pressure groups can use their 'power' very effectively – locally, nationally and globally ...

Paragraph 8
Surely it is wrong to see pressure groups as dangerous to democracy ...?

Task 5

Choose any three of the eight previous consecutive paragraphs and complete them, keeping the opening sentences as they are.

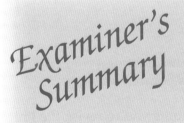

Examiner's Summary

- Argue against another viewpoint.
- Give special consideration to introductions and conclusions.
- Ensure, through your planning, that there is a logical structure and flow to your argument.

Unit 10 Revising Local Citizenship

Targets

1. Know what local government is responsible for.
2. Understand how decisions are made about your local area and how you can have a voice in the way that local democracy works.
3. Learn about ways to put your viewpoint across effectively.

Some facts about young people and local democracy

- There are around 13 million under-18-year-olds in the UK – nearly a quarter of the total population.
- Most local councils do not involve young citizens in the structures of local government.
- The qualification age for councillors is currently 21. While 50% of councillors are over 54, less than 10% are under 35.
- There is growing recognition of the rights of young people to participate and of the benefits of their involvement.
- Article 12 of the UN Convention on the Rights of the Child declares their 'right to be involved in all decisions concerning them'.

Citizenship education aims to give you the knowledge that you need to play a full part in society, including your local community. Local citizenship can operate at a school level. All schools have different ways in which students can make a difference, for example:

- painting social areas of the school
- making an environmental garden
- paired reading schemes with older students helping younger pupils
- projects where students work together to combat bullying.

Mostly, however, this Unit focuses upon helping you to revise the links between Citizenship Studies and the wider local community.

Task 1

Look at the ideas web on the following page:

a) Note down which services, buildings and types of people are found in your own community.

b) What evidence is there of 'shared values' in your local community?

FOCUS *Functions of local government*

c) What kinds of issues divide your community and generate strong feelings? How can these divisions be explained?
d) How does a local authority try to balance the competing interests of its citizens?

Things that local councils and councillors are responsible for:

Education   Sports centres   Housing   Fire fighting

Social services   Police   Rubbish collection   Transport

Roads (for example, repairs/gritting)   Council tax   Business rates

Pavements   Youth facilities (for example, skate parks)   Planning

---

Questions to think about

1. Why do you think local councils provide these services? What would happen if they did not provide them?
2. Who decides how much money to spend on each part of the council's work?

Skill 1: Identifying the features of local communities

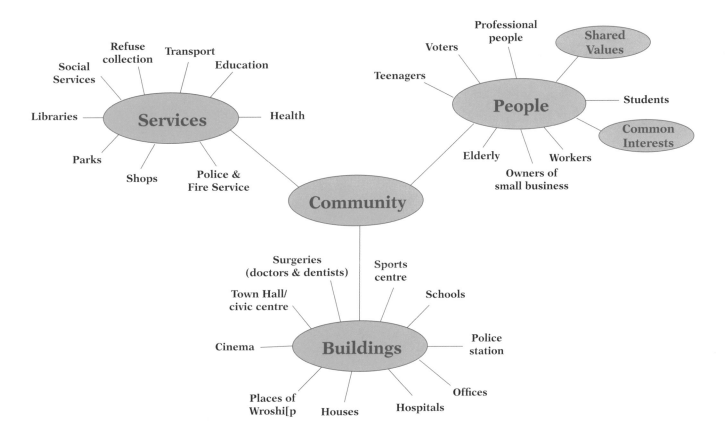

A community is made up of all the people who live in an area, as well as all the facilities and services in that area. You might live in an urban or a rural community. Different groups within an area will have different priorities. It is the role of local government to make decisions about local services and facilities and to manage them as efficiently as possible. Elected local councillors try to represent the views of their constituents and of their political parties.

Skill 2: Getting your voice heard

There are all sorts of things that you, or people in your school or local community, might want to change:

- A lack of wheelchair access – no ramps beside steps.
- People messing up your local environment.
- The closure of a local facility – a park, cinema or school.
- A lack of leisure facilities for young people.
- Cutbacks in the provision of buses to your local area.
- No re-cycling facilities.
- Speed of cars driving through your village.

Even people who are not old enough to vote can influence government decisions which affect them – especially at a local level. You can do this as an individual or by campaigning as a member of a voluntary or pressure group – a group of people who all have the same views can be more effective than one person campaigning alone.

> **Task 2**

Look at your local newspaper and find out about an issue that the council is discussing at the moment. What are the different points of view? What do you think? List three ways in which you might make your voice heard.

REMEMBER! Young people are citizens too. Think about the different ways in which you can make your voice heard in your school and community.

Task 3

Source A: Concrete proposal

Asked what they would like in their playground to replace the massive area of Tarmac and a single strip of grass, too dry in summer and too muddy in winter, the majority of children at a South London primary school proved surprisingly moderate in their demands – no duplicate Alton Towers, just a climbing frame, some monkey bars, more flowers, more shade, more quiet areas, more benches and a nature trail.

The older pupils said that while they were proud of what went on inside the building, they were ashamed of the impression the playground made on visitors.

A group of parents, supported by teachers, met to discuss what could be done. They opted not for a short-term fix of a couple of pieces of play equipment, benches, window boxes and repainting walls, but a long-term plan involving widespread consultation and fundraising.

[Adapted from *Guardian Education*, 4 September 2001]

a) **How realistic are the suggested improvements to the play area?**
b) **Who might oppose the proposals and why?**
d) **Think about and then list the different ways in which the primary school playground project might involve pupils, parents, staff and the local community in effective citizenship education.** (Look back at the key stage 4 *Citizenship National Curriculum* for ideas on this.)

Extension Work

This is a section from a local coursework project which would receive a top grade:

I've been a member of Billington Friends of the Earth (FoE) for 3 years and decided to base my project around my involvement with this environmental campaigning group. Ideas for action tend to come from within the group. As a charity we must avoid any party political involvement. We also have to make sure that we know our facts (for example, on transport issues we checked out the government's latest Green Paper, the Jubilee 2000 website, and the Council's 10-year transport plan).

We wanted to improve a 20-metre square plot of land next to the local community centre, which had a big pile of rubble on it, and turn it into a community garden. With three friends I set up a group called CAKE (Constructive Action in a Knackered Environment) – within this I was the marketing, fund-raising and publicity officer. Other roles included Site Manager; Community Centre and Council Liaison Officer and Treasurer/Secretary. We contacted all sorts of people asking for funding – we wanted to raise £2,000. I drafted and re-drafted letters very carefully and took a lot of advice from FoE and Youth Action Network on how to do this. Our biggest

continued …

achievement was to persuade the Council to 'match' any funds we raised ourselves. We received small grants from organisations such as the Lions Club, the local supermarket and the local bank. We also did our own fund-raising through a jumble sale and raffle …

Ten months later a beautiful garden got built but it was a much bigger and a more time-consuming task than we had thought at the start. I'm not unrealistic about grassroots action – it is difficult for a few people to change the world. But it is possible to change the local environment and make Local Agenda 21 a reality. If everyone put in a little bit of effort we could – at least by small steps – make the world a better place.

[Adapted from a news story in *GCSE Citizenship Studies* (Folens, 2001) p.79]

a) Write down the most effective examples of:
- **planning**
- **citizenship knowledge and understanding**
- **research**
- **organisation of the activity**
- **opinion/reflection/self-evaluation.**

b) What are the obstacles that make this kind of activity difficult?

c) Why do you think that the above project succeeded?

- Know the things that local government is responsible for.
- Research a topical issue in your local community.
- Take an active part in democratic processes and know how you can set about trying to change things.

Unit 11 *Revising National Citizenship*

Targets

1. Understand why Citizenship was introduced into the English school curriculum.
2. Know about how the parliamentary system works in the UK.
3. Develop a definition about what it means to be a British citizen.

Skill 1: What impact might Citizenship education have in terms of the way that young people think about politics?

There were many reasons why a government committee in 1998 recommended some big changes to the way in which Citizenship education was approached in schools. It found that:

- The majority of pupils did not have regular opportunities to discuss public issues.
- There was a decline in interest levels and participation in elections among the young.
- Some measures of youth alienation were increasing (for example, vandalism, petty crime, and anti-social behaviour).
- Basic information about democratic systems and international organisations was unknown to many young people.
- The media often had a negative influence in shaping attitudes towards politics.
- Society was changing at a faster pace than ever before, so young people needed to develop knowledge and skills to keep them ahead of these changes.
- Citizenship education, which helps young people understand concepts of identity and belonging, was also important in developing a full awareness of multicultural Britain.

We aim at no less than a change in the political culture of this country both nationally and locally ... for people to think of themselves as active citizens, willing, able and equipped to have an influence in public life, and with the critical capabilities to weigh evidence before speaking and acting; to build on and extend radically to young people ... the best in existing traditions of community involvement and public service, and to ... make them individually confident in finding new forms of involvement and activity among themselves. There are worrying levels of apathy, ignorance and cynicism about public life.

[*Education for Citizenship and the Teaching of Democracy in Schools*, September 1998]

What [Citizenship] is trying to do is teach young people about things like human rights, crime, sustainable development, and the fact that we live in a global society, so that we can make a change to some of the things that are going on in the world at the moment ... Citizenship is not about sitting in classrooms saying you must be good, you must vote ... The good part is the active bit ... This has the potential to be the most important subject on the curriculum. If there is engagement and empowerment between teachers and young people there may be opportunities to change society for future generations.

[Oli (17), contributing to a Radio 5 *Live Phone-in* on Citizenship, September 2002]

Task 1

Comment in about 500 words on the two views of Citizenship above. In your answer explain:

1. Why Citizenship was introduced to the National Curriculum in schools.
2. Why the two statements are optimistic about the possible effects of Citizenship education.
3. Whether you agree or disagree with the statements (and why).

Skill 2: Understanding how the parliamentary system works in the UK

There are a variety of things that you will find it helpful to know and think about:

- **How and why people vote for politicians**
- **Why fewer people are voting at elections**
- **How councillors, MPs and MEPs try to represent their constituents**
- **The Cabinet**
- **Different voting systems**
- **How laws are made by parliament**
- **The House of Lords**
- **The House of Commons**
- **The Prime Minister**
- **The budget**
- **General Elections**
- **The job of parliamentary committees**
- **Manifestos**
- **The ideas of the three main political parties (Labour, Conservatives, Liberal Democrats)**

After having done a lot of consultation, the Y Vote campaign (on the Hansard Society's HeadsUp website – www.headsup.org.uk) published the following agenda addressed by young people to politicians, the government and the media:

A young person's agenda for democracy

To politicians:

- Talk to us in language we can understand – simple, clear, basic; keep us informed.
- Talk to us directly, regularly, and in our environments – not just at election times, not just when we're old enough to vote, and face to face, not through a leaflet.
- Listen and respond to our concerns – don't lecture us and don't assume we have no opinions or you know what we think.
- Respect our diversity – and recognise that you need to find new ways of reaching out to different groups of young people.

To government:

- Give us the information and understanding we need – whether we are at school, college, work or even unemployed.
- Make citizenship education a priority within the curriculum – and give schools and colleges the support and resources they need to deliver it well.
- Seriously consider the arguments for lowering the voting age – and making voting compulsory, and making it easier to vote.

To the media:

- Make politics interesting and exciting for us – relate it to our lives but don't trivialise it with stories about politicians' private lives or political infighting – we are not interested.
- Find ways of mixing politics with entertainment – introduce political story lines into soaps, talk about political issues on chat shows, make it cool to be interested in politics.
- Use our interest in local issues – by giving us relevant, accurate and up-to-date information about local decision making and finding ways of involving us, asking our opinions, etc.

Task 2

Pick out four statements from the agenda above that you most strongly agree with. Explain your choices.

Skill 3: Knowing how laws are made

From the Hansard Society's HeadsUp website www.headsup.org.uk, an on-line forum for under 18-year-olds.

1. What happens before a new law is proposed?

- A green paper, may be written – this is when the general public is asked to give their views. It is also known as 'the consultation paper'.
- There will then be a 'white paper'. This is an outline of how the law will look.
- The proposed new law then becomes known as a 'Bill'.

2. How is a Bill introduced to MPs?

- A Bill can start in the House of Commons or the House of Lords.
- Normally a Bill will get its first reading in the House of Commons. This, basically, means giving MPs an outline of the Bill and then giving them time to prepare to debate the main issues of the Bill.

- A little while later, a Bill will get its second reading. This is when all MPs have an opportunity to debate and put forward the views of the people they represent.
- The next stage is the Committee Stage, when the Bill is debated clause by clause by a small group of MPs.
- The third reading is another chance for MPs to debate and then vote on whether they want the Bill to become law.

3. **What happens after MPs have voted for a Bill to become law?**
- The Bill is then debated in the House of Lords, where it follows the same stages. Members then also vote on whether the Bill is to become law. If the Bill has its first reading in the House of Lords the process is the same.
- The Bill is then sent back to the Commons for approval.
- The Bill is then presented to the Head of State – the Queen. The Queen, by tradition, will always pass a Bill that has been passed by Parliament.
- The Bill then becomes law.

Task 3

a) **What do you see as the good features of how laws are made by the British Parliament?**

b) **Can you see any problems with the process summarised here?**

c) **Find out who serves as members of the House of Lords.** Some people think that the House of Lords should be reformed and organised in a different way. What are the arguments for and against change?

Skill 4: Think about what makes you a British citizen

The concept of identity is at the heart of Citizenship Studies. However, the characteristics of 'Britishness', or indeed 'Englishness', are hard to pin down.

Factors which make shared sense of national identity hard to achieve

- The very concept of a nation state comes into question with the rise of international bodies (such as the European Union) and multinational companies (such as McDonald's or Microsoft).
- The political structures of the UK are changing rapidly. Devolution in Scotland, Wales and Northern Ireland has given Celtic peoples the freedom to promote their own nationality.
- Globally, and in Britain, mass migrations have mixed up populations and cultures.
- Most people have complex and multiple identities based upon loyalty to family, local community, religion, ethnicity, and gender, which contribute to a growing confusion in people's concept of national identity.
- There is cultural diversity. It is unlikely that there would be cultural harmony in a massive jamming session between London-based 'garage' musicians, Scottish pipers, a colliery brass band, drumming Orangemen from Northern Ireland, and a chamber orchestra – all of them distinctly British in their own way.

Task 4

Who are the British? In what ways are you British? Why do you feel proud to be British?

Source A: Lessons in 'Britishness'?

In December 2001 three reports identified racial segregation and isolation in Burnley, Oldham and Bradford as key factors leading to rioting. The Home Secretary, David Blunkett, called for minority ethnic groups to develop a new sense of Britishness:

We have to identify shared values that can unite the diverse communities in our towns and cities if people are to live and work together ... We have norms of acceptability and those who come into our home – for that is what it is – should accept those norms just as we would have to do if we went elsewhere ... If we are going to have social cohesion we have got to develop a sense of identity and a sense of belonging.

He was looking to promote common citizenship and considering making citizenship classes a condition of citizenship for new immigrants. For example, would-be citizens might be schooled in British democracy and culture and be obliged to learn English. There is no contradiction between retaining a distinct cultural identity and identifying with Britain. But our democracy must uphold fundamental rights and obligations to which all citizens and public authorities adhere. Citizenship means finding a common place for diverse cultures and beliefs, consistent with the core values we uphold.

These are not easy issues for our society to debate. [These issues] go to the heart of our beliefs and our identities.

[Adapted from the *Guardian*, 11 December 2001]

Source B: Is there a sense of British identity to unite around?

[Mr Blunkett] talks as though he has yet to learn that more than half of the non-white people who live in this country were born here. Second and third generations who have been trying to turn Britain from a house into a home are once again being shown the visitors' entrance ... Stephen Lawrence could speak better English than the thugs who killed him. And if anyone needed citizenship lessons it was the assailants' parents, who raised such hateful, racist criminals as children – not the determined, eloquent Neville and Doreen Lawrence. But at the heart of the problem lies not his lack of understanding of the experiences of blacks and Asians but his woefully simplistic notion of what it means to be British. He speaks of citizenship as though there is any consensus as to what 'citizenship' actually means in a nation of subjects to the Crown, without a written constitution and struggling with devolution, European integration, globalisation and the decline of the monarchy ... He wants new immigrants to sign up to an identity that those who have lived here for centuries cannot agree on.

[Gary Younge, 'Britain is white again', the *Guardian*, 18 February 2002]

Task 5

- What are Sources A and B disagreeing about?
- Who has responsibility for creating a sense of belonging?

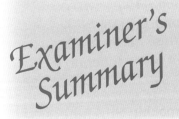

Examiner's Summary

- Understand what Citizenship education is trying to achieve.
- Know what parliament does and why it matters.
- Consider what it means to be a British citizen (and why this is hard to define).

Unit 12 *Revising Global Citizenship*

Targets

1. Consider what it means to be a global citizen and begin to understand the meaning of concepts such as interdependence, globalisation, and sustainability.
2. Know something about the role of international organisations such as the United Nations (UN) and the European Union (EU).

Skill 1: Beginning to understand what it means to live in a global village

We live together as members of neighbourhoods, communities, villages and towns, but also are part of a European and global community. The UK is a member of several international organisations including the UN, the EU, the Commonwealth, and NATO (North Atlantic Treaty Organisation). These memberships bring with them rights and responsibilities – but most people are comparatively ignorant of what they are.

> The fundamental challenge facing us today is one of connection. We can talk about global citizenship, but if people have little idea about the world in which they will become citizens, it is very difficult to turn the concept of citizenship into anything meaningful.
>
> [Jon Snow, Broadcaster, Channel 4 News at the Developing Global Citizens' Conference, 2000]

About one in five of the world's 1.2 billion population live in poverty, without adequate food, water, sanitation, healthcare or education for their children. And yet this is a time of increasing knowledge, technology. and capital, in the developed world. People in developed countries of the world account for only 20% of the world's population but they consume 86% of the world's total resources. If we do not do better in reducing inequality it is likely to lead to growing conflict, refugee movements, major environmental problems, disease and natural disasters.

Too often we lack the knowledge, understanding and skills that would enable us to think critically about global issues, make truly informed decisions and take appropriate action at a personal, local, national and international level about globalisation.

Ways in which the UK is connected to the rest of the world

- Trade
- Overseas aid
- Peacekeeping through the UN
- Acid rain
- Debt relief
- Membership of international organisations (UN, EU, NATO, Commonwealth)
- Global warming/climate change
- Impact of deforestation
- Place of refuge for asylum seekers
- Commitment to protecting human rights (the UK signed the UN Declaration of Human Rights)
- Agreement to implement Agenda 21 (UN Conference, Rio, 1992)
- Famine relief
- The UK is a permanent member of the UN Security Council
- Greenhouse gases

Task 1

Why should we care about what is happening elsewhere in the world? There are enough problems to worry about in Britain. Governments spend too much time and money on world affairs. People in other countries just want to take advantage of Britain's generosity.

Using your notes and the box above, explain in about 500 words why you think that this opinion is misinformed and how there is an interdependence between the UK and the rest of the world.

Skill 2: Understanding globalisation

Globalisation refers to the way in which business, politics, and culture operate on a world stage, not confined to single countries or continents. It has speeded up over the last 25 years:

- Technological changes have made communications throughout the world simpler and faster (for example, the Internet, e-mail).
- Lower costs and improved technology have led to a large increase in the movement of people and goods around the world (for example, cheap air fares).
- There has been rapid political change (for example, the collapse of the Soviet Union).
- Multinational companies (like Coca-Cola, McDonald's and Nike) have become much freer to move their operations and investments to different parts of the world.

The case for globalisation

Increasing international trade should help both the developed and developing world grow wealthier. Globalisation gives millions of people access to all sorts of goods and services. It improves standards of living in the world as a whole. For example, Japanese companies set up electronic factories and manufacturing plants in Britain. Zambian farmers send vegetables for sale in Britain.

The fall of protectionist barriers has stimulated free movement of money and enabled companies to set up several bases around the world. Governments generally see multinational companies as a force for good. They create work, spread wealth, introduce new technology, and help people to learn new ways of doing business. Many companies also work for the good of local communities, with projects to improve education, health, and the environment. The World Trade Organisation (WTO), formed in 1995 with 141 members, exists to police global trade and settle disputes between governments.

Linked to increased international travel, globalisation also promotes a better understanding of other cultures, as well as allowing consumers in the developed world more choice on the High Street. For the populations of developing countries, who sometimes live in extreme poverty, it is the best chance they have of improving their lifestyles. Developing countries want the investment from multinational companies. The opposition of anti-capitalist protesters to globalisation and free trade make them an enemy of the world's poor.

The case against globalisation

The gain for developed countries has been at the expense of the developing world. Multinational companies set up factories or operations in less developed countries to take advantage of cheaper labour or a supply of raw materials. Some companies are criticised for offering much poorer pay and working conditions to workers overseas than they do at home. Even in the developed world, not everyone has been a winner. Globalisation has increased insecurity in the workplace. Workers are under threat as companies shift their businesses to lower-wage economies (for example, the closure of call centres in the UK and their switch to India).

Although governments usually welcome foreign investment in their country, the benefits can be short-lived. Promises of jobs sometimes mean that measures to protect the environment are ignored. The globalisation model allows businesses to be unregulated and beyond the reach of government powers. Businesses that do have ethical standards find themselves competing at a disadvantage with the majority of companies that do not. The WTO and the World Bank tend to support the interests of big business rather than the needs of ordinary people.

Too many foreign imports damage a country's industry and culture. Giant companies squeeze out local producers and limit choice. Different approaches are needed that emphasise on reducing poverty, sustaining the environment and maintaining human rights.

FOCUS

Globalisation

Task 2

Use the information above to draft two 150-word statements for a press conference. One is to answer charges that conditions for World Trade are shaped at the expense of the developing world, the other from a pressure group setting out the potential dangers of globalisation.

Skill 3: What is meant by 'sustainable development'?

The students currently in schools and colleges are those who will decide whether Homo sapiens makes it beyond 2100. If the next generation of young people don't get the message about the way the planet is heading, and act on the information, the future looks bleak … The threats facing the planet are well documented … Whether it is climate change, destruction of rainforests, the spread of deserts, loss of species, or the lack of clean water, the root cause is humankind's over-use and misuse of limited resources.

Eleven years ago, at the first Earth Summit in Rio, this message got into the political system. But for the politicians it was inconvenient that carrying on as we are was no longer possible. To do something about it would cost votes.

All we apparently needed was 'sustainable development' and the world would be saved. The concept was not really understood, still less acted upon, apart from by a few enthusiasts. At the second Earth Summit in Johannesburg in 2002 everyone agreed that matters had gone downhill fast since 1992 and the problems were accelerating.

Some of the problems of sustainable development can be seen at the Blackwater Estuary in Essex. It is an area where humans mainly control the environment, and is responsible for varied uses of the land and the sea. There are water and land pollution issues, and conflicts between shipping, tourism, and recreational and commercial fishing. In addition to this, the forces of nature (made more extreme by our attack on the climate) are altering the coastline with storms and a rise in the level of the sea. One question here is whether land reclaimed long ago should be allowed to turn back into salt marsh to provide habitat for fish and birds, and at the same time to provide protection from the sea. There are conflicting interests between farmers, fishermen and town dwellers, all of whom have different ideas .

The Blackwater example is a good case study because, unlike most areas of environmental crisis, the people of the area have got together and come up with solutions as to the best way to share the resource, and reduce dangers to and from nature … It shows that once people understand the problems, it is possible to find compromises and solutions. Despite the conflicting economic and emotional issues, the equally important message is that doing nothing is not an option.

[Adapted and abridged from Paul Brown, 'What on Earth', *Guardian Education*, 6 May 2003]

Sustainable development: definitions

Development which meets the needs of the present without compromising the ability of future generations to meet their own needs.

Sustainable development:
- protects the planet's water, air and soil and looks to develop alternative sources of energy
- values all people and species
- promotes local solutions to problems.

Task 3

a) **Organisations such as Comic Relief, Oxfam, Christian Aid, CAFOD, and many more, sponsor sustainable development projects. Research the international work of one or more of these organisations** through their internet websites and identify two to three problems that they have addressed and the solutions that they and their local partners came up with.

b) **Write a 250-word critical commentary on the above newspaper article** (p.75) from *Guardian Education* on sustainable development. Use evidence from your textbook and class notes to support your commentary. (Think about its content, tone, and overall message.)

Skill 4: The role of the United Nations and the European Union

FOCUS

The United Nations and the European Union

The UN and the EU are often in the news – usually when there are major world problems to address or when there is a disagreement between Britain and other countries about particular policies. The big question to think about is why should you care about international issues and the work of organisations such as the UN and the EU. Many people are critical of the work that they do. The UN has certainly struggled since the Second World War in its main task to resolve conflicts and keep the peace between countries. There are regular arguments within the EU about different policies and the UK government often tends to be cautious about proposals for members of the EU to work more closely with other European countries. These organisations however, also do a lot of important work which is not so well publicised.

Task 4

a) Look at your notes, textbook, and current newspaper stories. **Draw up a balance sheet of positive things about the work of the UN and EU, and problems and difficulties.**

	Positive aspects of their work	Problems and difficulties
United Nations		
European Union		

b) Using the Internet (for example, www.una-uk.org or www.unayouth.org.uk), an encyclopaedia, and your notes, **name four organizations within the UN**.

- **Write 50–75 words about what each organisation does.**
- **Find out what one of these organisations is currently dealing with and write a brief description of its activities in relation to this issue.**
- **Which of the four organisations do you think is most important and why?**

There are perhaps three main questions you need to have some answers to in relation to the EU:

1. What is the point of the EU and how is it organised?

2. How does membership of the EU affect the lives of ordinary people in Britain?

3. Why do some British people have strong opinions for and against the EU? A good place to start (and to have your say if you have a strong opinion) is www.citizen.org.uk/speakout, an Institute for Citizenship information and discussion site for young people focusing on European Citizenship. The Foreign Office website, www.europeday.gov.uk, also has some useful information about Britain and the EU.

Task 5

a) Find out which European constituency you are in and the name of your Member of the European Parliament (MEP). How has Britain's membership of the EU affected life in your area?

b) Talk to friends, relatives, and teachers. What does European citizenship mean to people you know? Would they describe themselves as European?

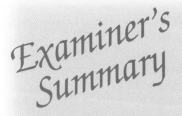

Examiner's Summary

- Understand issues arising from global interdependence, globalisation, and national responsibility for global issues such as the question of sustainability.
- Know about the UK's role in global organisations, including the EU and the UN, and how these organisations are structured and allow for participation.
- Be able to write about the power of active citizens in relation to global affairs (for example, as consumers, members of pressure groups, supporters of voluntary agencies or voters).

Unit 13 *Citizenship and the Law*

Targets

1. Understand how the law affects you in aspects of everyday life.
2. Understand the function of different parts of the legal system.
3. Recognise how and why attitudes towards law and order are controversial.

Legal rules influence many aspects of your life. A lot of the work that you will have done in Citizenship Studies concerns questions of fairness, justice or rights. Specifically, for your Citizenship Studies examination you will need to be able to explain and analyse:

- How the lives of young people and adults are affected by the law, including consumer, race relations, human rights, and age-related legislation. [For more detail on Human Rights see Unit 8.]
- How laws are made and how courts at local, national, and European levels exercise their power and authority.
- The difference between criminal and civil law and the role of key people in the legal system, including the police, magistrates, solicitors, barristers, judges and juries – with the help of case studies.
- Why there can be disagreement about how to tackle crime and punish criminals.
- How individuals and groups can make changes to laws through campaigning.

Skill 1: Understanding the different parts of the legal system

---

Law processes in England and Wales

- Laws are created and developed by **Parliament** (statute law), by **judges** in courts (case law), and through the UK's links with Europe. The police enforce criminal laws.
- The organisation of the courts of England and Wales is designed to provide speedy and efficient justice for all people involved in the criminal justice system. In the interests of efficiency the overwhelming majority of cases (about 98%) are heard locally by **lay magistrates** in **magistrates courts** (for example, speeding and vandalism). In some cases the accused can opt for trial by his peers – by **jury**. This would take place in a **Crown Court**.
- More serious cases (for example, murder or rape) are tried in **Crown courts**.
- Prosecutions are brought by an independent **barrister** for the **Crown Prosecution Service** (CPS). The CPS decides if there is enough evidence to bring a case to court. The judge has no role in directly collecting evidence as to guilt or innocence. He or she acts as a referee and interpreter of the law. It is for a 12-person jury to decide whether guilt has been proved beyond reasonable doubt on the basis of the evidence presented.
- **Civil Courts** deal with disputes other than criminal (for example, divorce, compensation claims from shops, and disagreements about property or tax law). There are **Tribunals** for specific areas of law, such as social security and employment, as well as informal court procedures dealing with small claims.

Task 1

Explain the role of each of the institutions or jobs highlighted in bold in the above box (p.78). (Write at least two sentences in each case.)

Skill 2: Knowing how the law affects you in everyday life

What legal rights do you have as a consumer?

What kind of laws affect shops and pubs?

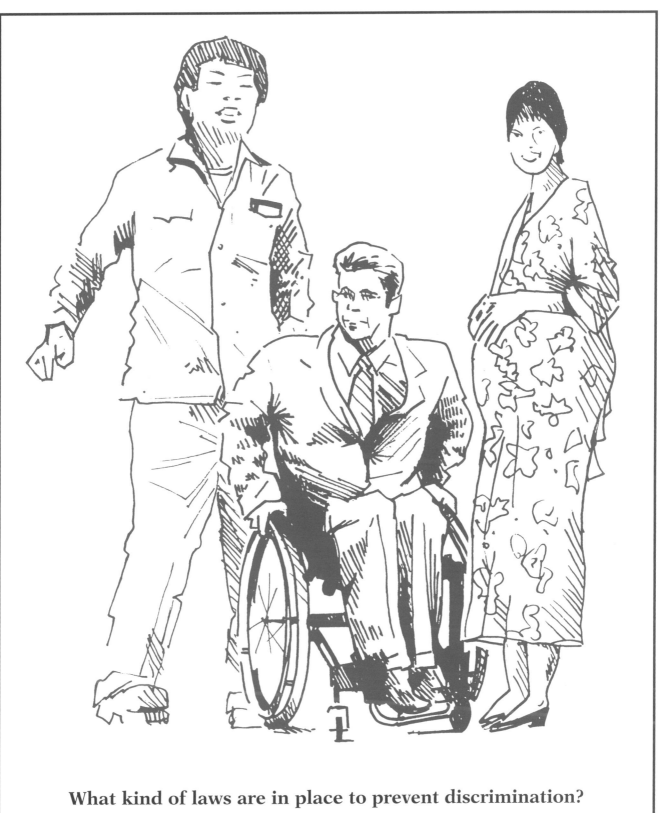

What kind of laws are in place to prevent discrimination?

What are the legal rights of workers?

FOCUS
The law and everyday life

Task 2

a) Look at each of the pictures on the previous pages and draw up a list of some of the laws that apply to each of the situations shown. (Some answers are on p.85 – but see what you think before you look at them.)

b) Can you think of any laws that you disagree with? Explain why. Should people obey laws that they disagree with?

Skill 3: Law and order: the big debates

FOCUS
Crime and punishment

It is too easy to simplify debates about crime to conflicts between two opposing points of view. One side of the debate offers a tough approach and emphasises personal responsibility, the feelings of victims of crime, and the encouragement of self-discipline. The tough approach also supports more policemen and police powers and heavier punishment and imprisonment for convicted criminals.

The other side of the debate points to the conditions which result in people committing crimes, such as unemployment, poverty, and poor education, and states that some compassion should be shown towards criminals. The liberal approach argues that in the UK too many people end up in prison, prison rarely works, and that the legal system should put more emphasis on reform than punishment. Is it possible that there is some truth in both these points of view?

Task 3

In 1996, before he was elected as Prime Minister, Tony Blair promised to be 'tough on crime and tough on the causes of crime.'

a) Think of four policies which might demonstrate that a government is 'tough on crime'.

b) How can politicians act to reduce the causes of crime?

c) Do you think that too many people are imprisoned in the UK? Give reasons for your answer. (You may want to research the figures for crime and punishment in the UK over the past 5 years. Look at the website of the Office for National Statistics, www.statistics.gov.uk, or the British Crime Survey, www.homeoffice.gov.uk).

New survey reveals extent of crime against 12- to 16-year-olds

One in four young people aged 12 to 16 has been a victim of crime in the last year, according to research published [February 2003] by Victim Support. The survey marks the start of a campaign to introduce nationwide support services for all young people who have been affected by crime. The research, carried out on over 400 young people across England and Wales, reveals some worrying trends.

- It suggests that the level of crime against this age group is consistent over time (similar numbers said the crime was up to three, six or twelve months ago), widespread, and that it affects both boys and girls equally.
- Almost half (42%) of those who have been victims had been subjected to repeat incidents.
- The most common offences reported included violence and assault (54%), or theft (43%); 5% said that it was a sexual offence. Only 2% of victims specifically reported a mobile phone-related crime, but many more who said that they had been a victim of theft or robbery could have been the victim of phone theft.

'This survey highlights the extent to which crime is now affecting young people and strengthens our case for extending our work to offer specialist help for this age group,' said Peter Dunn, Head of Research and Development at Victim Support. The charity plans to launch a number of pilot schemes for young victims around the country later this year.

[Victim Support, www.victimsupport.org]

Task 4

a) How would you feel if you were the victim of some of the crimes highlighted here? What kind of support would young people find useful?

b) Explain the process, step by step, of how the criminal justice system would deal with someone accused of a serious theft after an allegation has been made to the police.

c) How tough would you be in your sentencing of someone convicted of stealing a mobile phone?

Skill 4: Citizens and the law

FOCUS

Individual citizens and the law

An excellent guide to the law is the *Young Citizen's Passport* (Hodder and Stoughton), produced by the Citizenship Foundation and specially designed for young people. There should be a copy of this in your school or library. It is updated every year and is supported by two websites: www.teachingcitizenship.co.uk and www.citfou.org.uk.

Task 5

When you think about the relationship between individuals and the law, there are some potentially big and difficult questions to consider.

Activate your revision by talking about it

EXAMINER'S TIP!

Look at the questions below and think of three possible answers and responses. For each of your three points then think about and develop at least two pieces of evidence, examples or case studies to support your conclusions. Here you have a chance to make your revision a bit more active – try out some of the questions below on friends and relatives – you should collect a range of different ideas and opinions.

- What would life be like without laws?
- Why might some people have a negative view of the law?
- Do you think that we, as citizens, should be more actively involved in shaping the laws of this country?
- What changes might be made to the workings of our courts and legal system to make the law more accessible to the ordinary citizen?
- Some people feel that judges are not sufficiently in touch with ordinary people. One Lord Chancellor said that he would like to change this. What suggestions would you make to ensure that judges have more understanding of the lives of people in Britain?

Answers

Task 2

1. You have certain basic legal rights when you buy goods or services. Shops have a legal obligation to replace a faulty kettle or toaster or refund customers if they are not of satisfactory quality under the **Sale of Goods Act** (1979).
2. The **Consumer Protection Act** (1987) made it an offence to mislead customers about the price of goods. Goods also need to fit the description used in any labelling. Pub owners are governed by licensing laws which detail when they can open. It is illegal to sell alcoholic drinks to under 16s.
3. Several laws make it unlawful to discriminate against individuals on the grounds of disability, sex, race, colour or ethnic origin, for example, the **Race Relations Act** (1975); **Sex Discrimination Acts** of 1975 and 1986; the **Disability Discrimination Act** (1995). Maternity rights have improved recently, bringing UK law in line with European legislation.
4. The **Health and Safety at Work Act** (1974) aims to ensure safe and healthy working conditions.

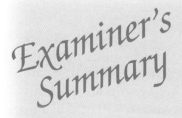
Examiner's Summary

- Know about the role and operation of the criminal justice system.
- Revise the rights and responsibilities of consumers, employers, and employees.
- Decide what your opinions are on some of the big debates that relate to law and order and then back up your opinions with evidence and examples.

Unit 14 *Citizenship Studies Links with Other Subject Areas*

Skill 1: Recognising areas where you have transferable knowledge and skills

FOCUS
Identifying Citizenship links with other subjects

Some of the knowledge and skills that you are revising for your other GCSE courses could also be used in the context of your Citizenship Studies work. It is worth checking out whether you can revise two subjects for the price of one!

This Unit will help you to explore the links with GCSE English, History, RE, and Geography in a bit more detail, however, but other subjects may also be relevant, for example, science in society investigations; the issue of fairness and the effectiveness of rules in sport; exploring controversial issues in Media Studies; debates within your PSHE work.

Task 1

Create a diagram something like the one on the following page (yours will be different depending upon your choices of GCSE subjects) and **work out where there is an overlap between what you have been studying in other subjects and your GCSE Citizenship Studies work**.

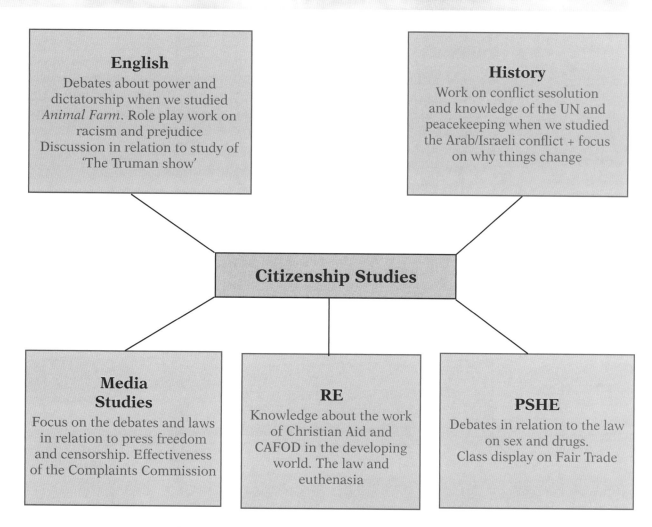

English
Debates about power and dictatorship when we studied *Animal Farm*. Role play work on racism and prejudice Discussion in relation to study of 'The Truman show'

History
Work on conflict sesolution and knowledge of the UN and peacekeeping when we studied the Arab/Israeli conflict + focus on why things change

Citizenship Studies

Media Studies
Focus on the debates and laws in relation to press freedom and censorship. Effectiveness of the Complaints Commission

RE
Knowledge about the work of Christian Aid and CAFOD in the developing world. The law and euthenasia

PSHE
Debates in relation to the law on sex and drugs. Class display on Fair Trade

Skill 2: Making links between Citizenship Studies and English

At key stage 4, English is the core subject that has the closest links with Citizenship Studies. As part of your work in GCSE English you will have been developing skills of enquiry and communication and participation and responsible action which are key tools for effective and active Citizenship. For example, your English teachers will have asked you to 'justify an argument orally and in writing', 'contribute to discussions', 'use your imagination to put yourself in the shoes of other people', 'negotiate', 'decide', and 'reflect'. You might also have been asked to 'research' and 'formally debate' particular topics. You may have taken part in role-play simulations.

The English department also contributes to Citizenship in the area of knowledge and understanding. Human rights, identities, prejudice and discrimination probably figured as themes in books you have studied. Work on media and moving images (including ICT-based sources) links closely with the wider demands of Citizenship's study of the media in society. The importance of a free press and the role of the media have occurred in one way or another as part of the GCSE language examination on many occasions in the past ten years and the topic is likely to be practice material in Year 11, making it doubly useful.

Task 2

a) Look at the diagram below and consider the various parties involved in making the world a better place for children. Put these in rank order. Think of a factor that you might add in the blank bubble. Justify your view to a friend, relative or teacher.

b) Write two paragraphs, or create a collage of images and words, to answer the question 'If the world became a better place for children what would it look like?'

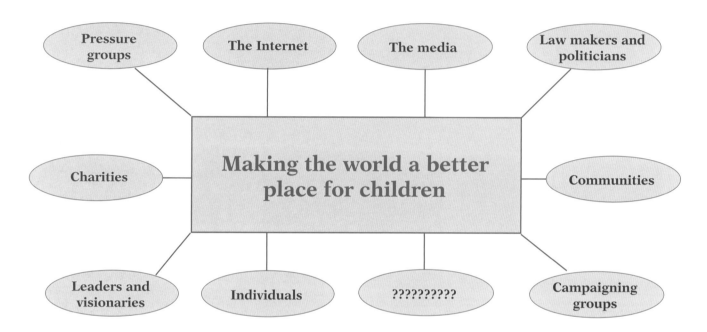

Skill 3: Making links between Citizenship Studies and History

History is a good subject to help you understand the political literacy aspects of Citizenship Studies. The making of the United Kingdom, the changing relationship between monarchy, parliament and people, and the relative powers of central and local government are key themes within the three British History core study units you have studied in Years 7–9 covering the years 1066–1900. All human societies have faced the dilemma of generally needing some degree of freedom of choice but also needing to live together and accept restrictions. History contains many examples of attempts to resolve this dilemma and events where rights and responsibilities have clashed. You might have studied the Peasants' Revolt, the English Civil War, Peterloo and the Chartist Movement, and the Suffragettes. There are lots of historical examples here of different methods of popular protest and bringing about change.

Task 3

Combining your History knowledge and your Citizenship notes and reading, ask yourself at what point you think that defiance of the law becomes legitimate. (The activities of fuel protesters and anti-capitalist protesters in recent times are contemporary examples.) Give three examples where you think that defiance of the law was legitimate and three examples where you disagree with the form of protest. Justify your arguments.

Twentieth-century History studied in Year 9, and often at GCSE level as part of 'Modern World' syllabuses, brings many Citizenship issues to the History curriculum. In studying, for example, the two World Wars, the Cold War, totalitarian regimes such as Hitler's Germany or Stalin's Russia, the 'Homefront' in Britain in the 1914–18 and 1939–45 conflicts, and defining episodes of the twentieth century such as the Holocaust and the dropping of atomic bombs on Hiroshima and Nagasaki, there are opportunities for analysing fundamental moral and political questions.

Task 4

If you are studying Nazi Germany in the 1930s for your History GCSE you may be asked: 'How did Hitler establish totalitarian control over German society after 1933?'

To answer this question you will need to consider: the Enabling Act and an end to elections after March 1933; the use of appointed Nazi *gauleiters* to run local government; the control of the Army and judges; a dictated school curriculum; the imprisonment of political opponents; the use of an unaccountable police force to terrorise German society – the SA and the SS; the issuing of many Nazi laws (for example, the Nuremburg Laws); censorship of the press and the use of propaganda; the oppression of minorities – not only Jews but gypsies, homosexuals and Jehovah's Witnesses. **Now try drafting an answer.**

Look at this Citizenship Studies question:
'What rights and freedoms do individual citizens enjoy in democratic society?'

If you reverse some of the arguments used in your Nazi Germany answer you will have identified some of the areas that you need to talk about in exploring the relationship between individuals and the state. If you are asked a question about democracy or rights you can gain credit from examiners for using relevant historical examples to support your opinions. See if you can write at least a side of A4 on the above question – you may be able to manage more than this if your revision has been going well.

Skill 4: Making links between Citizenship Studies and RE

There is an overlap between Citizenship Studies and RE in several areas. For example, in terms of content in both subjects you might have explored moral and social issues, including:

- prejudice, discrimination and inequality
- issues related to war and peace and the resolution of conflicts
- medical ethics and the law in relation to, for example, abortion and euthanasia
- the work of religious charities and voluntary organisations
- the environment.

Through your study of RE you will also have developed skills useful to your GCSE Citizenship Studies course, in particular:

- An ability to explain and understand other people's points of view and explain the reasons for different opinions.
- Giving evidence and examples to make sure that your opinions are informed opinions.

Task 5

Religious believers might choose to support an environmental organisation because of their beliefs. For example, a Christian might support the Worldwide Fund for Nature because of his or her belief that people have a responsibility to be 'Stewards of the Earth'. As well as joining a charitable organisation, there are many ways in which religious believers might put their beliefs into practise in caring for the environment.

List and explain six actions that they might take – not only as religious believers but as responsible citizens.

Skill 5: Making Links between Geography and Citizenship Studies

Geography aims to help your understanding of the world as a global community, including an appreciation of different cultures and societies and an understanding of other peoples' values. (See Unit 13 for more ideas on global citizenship.) You will probably have had opportunities to explore contemporary social, environmental, economic, and political issues such as the giving of overseas aid in Geography lessons. You may also have studied environmental change and sustainable development through issues like deforestation or soil erosion, recognising the implications of these processes for people, places, and environments. Many projects designed to develop your skills in Geography can be duplicated as Citizenship topics (for example, gathering views and factual evidence about a local issue and using them to reach a conclusion).

Task 6

A water company wants to build a reservoir to provide a better water supply to a nearby town with an increasing population. Consider the views of the following groups affected by the company's plan: farmers; villagers – compulsorily re-housed; town residents; environmental campaigners; local councillors; water-sports company; laundry owners in the town; the local press.

Why might the proposal be controversial?
Who decides whether the water company can build the reservoir?

Examiner's Summary

- Recognise the links between Citizenship Studies and your work in other GCSE subjects.
- Practise using the relevant knowledge and skills that you have developed in other subjects in your Citizenship Studies work.

Unit 15 *Final Revision for Citizenship Studies*

Targets

1. To be well prepared to answer the examination paper.
2. To focus on what is being tested.
3. To understand the skills required for success.

This unit deals with the period leading up to the examination, and last-minute revision.

General Advice

1 **Revise the key Citizenship words and concepts that you need to know in order to answer shorter questions which call for definitions.**

Make sure you know:
- the meaning of technical Citizenship terms (for example, referendum, petition, lobby, etc.)
- the correct spellings
- how to use the words in sentences.

2 **Make sense of your notes**
- Read back over your homework and classwork. Look carefully at your teacher's comments. He/she will have told you when and where you have not put enough detail in your answers or are wandering off the point, so really make sure you understand where this is happening. There are a number of ways in which you might try to 'digest' your notes.
- It is a good thing, when you are revising, to do things with your notes – not just stare at them in an attempt to memorise, for example, go through your notes with a highlighter pen, picking out only the most important details and big points. Then take a postcard and as bullet points note these details under headings. If you learn those details as a skeleton, you will find that once you have read your notes through, you can begin to put some of the flesh on the skeleton, for example, you might try to put all of the material for one topic onto one page so that you can use it as a checklist. It can be useful to arrange it into a spidergram.
- The process of organising your notes and physically playing with ideas and information should help you to remember things better. Revising like this will also help you to identify gaps in your knowledge.

3 Make it fun, and vary how you revise

Don't just sit looking at your notes and trying to remember everything that you know you have learned about a topic – it doesn't work and gets deeply boring.

- Pair up with a friend or fellow student and write a revision quiz for him or her on a topic you both want to revise; in the meantime, he or she can do the same for you. Swap quizzes; by the time you have written and done one quiz and answered another you will be surprised how much has stuck in your memory.
- Try picking a topic that you found dull in class and finding a way of making it exciting. Perhaps search the Internet to find out about it in a different way. (Ask your teacher if they know of some good sites to save unnecessary 'surfing'.)
- Set yourself mini-targets for revision – for example, 'This morning I am going to learn about how and why Britain gets involved in European and world affairs, and I'll do a past question on it under timed conditions tomorrow.'
- Take regular short breaks to refresh yourself. Nobody can concentrate for hours on end. Get up and stretch your legs and perhaps even take some exercise. This helps to stimulate the brain. Have a drink – your brain also needs water.

Active revision activities, where you keep re-organising information and ideas, are more effective than passive attempts to memorise things.

EXAMINER'S TIP!

4 Write proper answers from your notes

- It is much better to answer a question by writing the answer out in full sentences. Usually examiners will only award up to half marks if a question is answered in note form.
- Revise around examination questions. Ask your teacher to give you a list of questions from past papers and use these to organise your revision. Take note of the exact wording of the questions.
- Look at your notes and write down the main points you want to put into the answer and then write the answer using only those points.

5 Use your time wisely in the examination

- Check how many marks are given for each question and divide up your time accordingly. The different examination boards vary on the number of marks allocated to the Citizenship Studies examination (AQA – 120; Edexcel – 80; OCR – 65). In the end, though, your examination performance will add up to 60% of your total mark for all the examination boards.
- For AQA and OCR the examination is 1 hour and 30 minutes; for Edexcel the paper is 1 hour and 15 minutes.
- When you have worked out how much time you get for each section and each question (your teacher will help you with this) try timing yourself to get an idea of how long you should be spending on each one. Whenever you make a point, prove it.
- Obviously, you should try to spend as much time as possible on questions with the largest numbers of marks. In the case of Citizenship Studies this is the long essay at the end of the paper.

6 Avoid making silly and unnecessary mistakes

- Make sure that you turn up on the right day in the right place to take the examination and that you have all the equipment that you need (including a spare pen).
- Read the written extracts and other sources carefully.
- Answer what is asked. Divide your time sensibly between different sections of the paper.
- Leave time to check your answers at the end, improve your grammar and look for misspellings. It might gain you an extra mark or two.

Understanding levels of response mark schemes

It is disheartening to read an answer from a candidate who obviously knows their stuff subject, with details pouring out, but who has not answered the actual question. Ask your teacher for a copy of the Mark Scheme for last year's paper. This is sent to all schools. You will see that a 15-mark question is divided into 5 Levels. A typical 15-mark question might be:

'There is too much emphasis on the rights of British citizens and not enough emphasis on their responsibilities and duties.' Write an essay to show how far you agree with this statement. (15 marks)

In your answer you may use examples from your studies and from your own experience and local area.

First, underline the key/command words. What does this question want you to do, and what does it not want you to do?

The mark scheme for this might look something like the following:

Level 1: Candidate offers a simple reaction to the statement, with some limited but relevant evidence/examples. *(one–three marks)*

Level 2: Candidate offers a reaction to the statement and demonstrates some understanding of the different dimensions of the issue, for example, supported agreement OR supported disagreement. A few relevant examples – largely descriptive and undeveloped – are given of citizens' rights and responsibilities. *(four–six marks)*

Level 3: Candidate offers a limited evaluation of the statement, with reference to knowledge from their studies and personal experience. A fairly clear structure. Includes relevant examples of citizens' rights and responsibilities with some development. *(seven–nine marks)*

Level 4: Candidate offers a detailed, structured evaluation of the statement, with a logical conclusion. Points for and against the statement are often supported by relevant and detailed examples, with recognition of the alternative viewpoint. *(ten–twelve marks)*

Level 5: An excellent account which fully answers the question. Candidates offer a convincing evaluation, with a well-argued conclusion. Candidates understand the balance and inter-relationship between rights and responsibilities. They reflect thoughtfully on their own experience and provide good local examples. *(thirteen–fifteen marks)*

If you only agree or disagree with the title, and give a few reasons, you only reach Level 2, probably five marks. The same if you just disagree. But if you discuss rights and responsibilities and include some relevant examples you are into Level 3 and can secure nine marks. So the rule is: **always balance your answer**. Now, if you start to bring in a wider range of examples from your studies and specific local material that you know about, give your opinion and reach a conclusion, you can reach Level 4 or even 5, which is 10–15 marks. This is not easy to do in timed conditions, but examiners want you to do well. They are encouraged to mark positively and will applaud your efforts to analyse and not simply describe.

You need to know things on topics like Democracy in Britain; Human Rights; Global Citizenship, and the Freedom of the Press. In-depth means that you support arguments with plenty of specific detail.

You need to know about how Citizenship in action works, with case studies from your own local area. Find examples of how individuals, voluntary groups or pressure groups have made a difference and brought about change.

Characteristics of Grade A qualities for GCSE Citizenship Studies

You demonstrate in-depth knowledge and understanding about rights and responsibilities, communities and identities, democracy and government and the impact these have on societies, culture and the global community.

- *You do this by drawing on specific examples and explaining the meaning and importance of Citizenship issues in relation to your own and other people's lives and communities.*
- *You discuss, interpret and evaluate a variety of different responses demonstrating an appreciation of others' points of view.*
- *You recognise the complexity of issues studied, weigh up opinions and make judgements supported by a range of evidence and well-developed arguments.*
- *You critically evaluate your participation in school and/or community-based activities, providing evidence of your abilities to work with others.*
- *You show that you can make a range of contributions to group decision-making and assess the effects of your participation.*
- *You have negotiated your roles and responsibilities within project work groups and facilitated the participation of others.*

If you recognise the complexity of issues, you realise that things happen for a number of reasons and there are rarely easy answers. There are likely to be a number of possible solutions to problems – your job is to evaluate (for example, look at the pros and cons) different options. Arguments will be well developed if you support your ideas with examples and evidence.

You have undertaken a Citizenship project. You have also researched and evaluated it. What went well and why? What could have been improved and how?

You have got fully involved and can explain how you worked with others and how your involvement made a difference.

Examiner's Summary

- Good luck in your Citizenship Studies examination and coursework – I hope that you have found some of the advice and information in this book helpful.

Maths
made easy

Preschool
ages 3-5
Matching and Sorting

Author and Consultant
Su Hurrell

LONDON • NEW YORK • MUNICH • MELBOURNE • DELHI

Not the same

Draw a (ring) round the animal that is not the same.

Draw 2 animals that are not the same.

Not the same

Draw a (ring) round the sock that is different.

Draw a (ring) round the glove that is different.

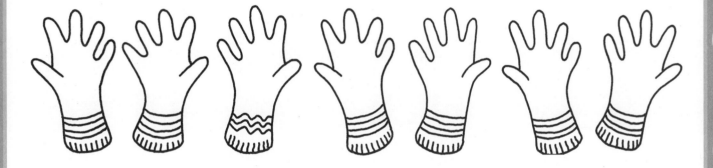

Draw a sock that is different.   Draw a glove that is different.

Different

Draw a (ring) round the flag that is different.

Draw the flag that is different.

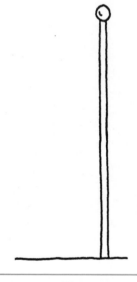

Draw what it should look like.

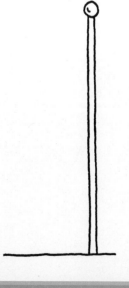

Different numbers

Count how many spots on the big ladybird.

Draw a (ring) round the ladybird with
a different number of spots.

Draw a (ring) round the ladybird with
a different number of spots.

Different numbers

Draw a different number of shapes on the umbrellas.

The same

Match the animals.

Draw and colour **2** animals that are the same.

The same

Draw lines to match the shoes that are the same. Make pairs.

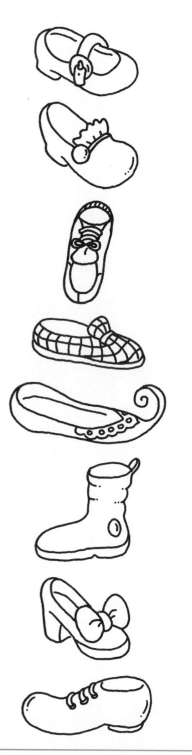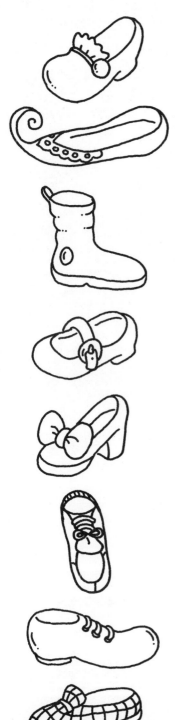

Draw a pair of shoes for yourself.

The same

Find the big triangles △. Colour them red.
Find the small circles ○. Colour them blue.

Count how many red triangles.

Count how many blue circles.

The same

Draw lines to match the monsters.

The same

Draw the other half to match.
Use a mirror to help you.

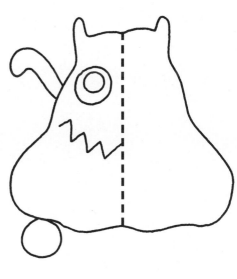

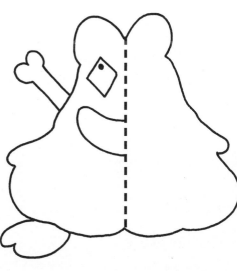

Sorting sets
Draw a line to the right set.

Count how
many altogether.

Count how
many altogether.

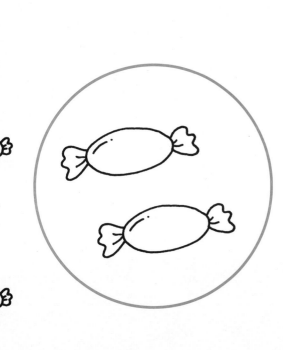

Count how
many altogether.

Count how
many altogether.

Adding to sets

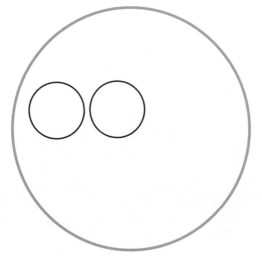

Draw **2** more.
Count how many
in the set.

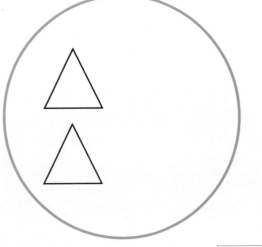

Draw **1** more.
Count how many
in the set.

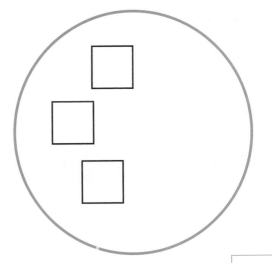

Draw **3** more.
Count how many
in the set.

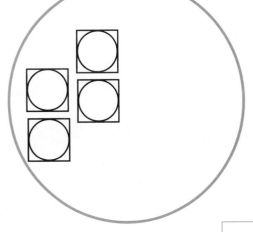

Draw **4** more.
Count how many
in the set.

Draw a set of **6** triangles.

Sorting the toys

Look at the toys in the circles.
Match the other toys to the right circle.

Sorting the trees

Count how many apples on each tree.

How many trees have...

3 apples		4 apples		5 apples	

Draw 1 more tree for each set.

Now how many trees have...

3 apples		4 apples		5 apples	

15

Sorting the animals
Look at the animals. Count how many legs.
Match them to the right part of the Ark.

2 legs

0 legs

4 legs

6 legs

Notes for parents

During play activities, children frequently match, sort, create patterns, and talk about sequences. This book reinforces and establishes those concepts and skills in a fun and enjoyable way.

The book includes some counting and number matching, so your child should be familiar with the numbers and quantities up to 10. Shapes and colours are also included in some activities.

Content

By working through this book your child will learn:
- to look closely at shapes, objects, and patterns;
- to match;
- to identify similarities and differences;
- to sort things into sets;
- to use more than one criterion for this sorting process;
- to add to sets and count the total;
- to recognise what a pattern is;
- to continue patterns and create them;
- to understand the concept of before and after;
- to put events in the right sequential order;
- to use ordinal numbers correctly;
- to complete sequences.

How to help your child

A child learns through hands-on experiences so it is important your child has had a range of practical experiences before attempting the activities in the book.

This book is designed to be an enjoyable experience for both you and your child, a shared time together. Make sure that your child is alert and not too tired. Keep the time spent appropriate to the age and level of concentration of your child.

The pages are designed for your child to colour, which develops pencil control, eye and hand co-ordination, and builds up concentration. Make sure there is a range of coloured pencils or felt-tip pens available.

Talk about the activities on each page and make sure your child understands what they are to do.

Remember this book is for fun as well as being educational, so stop before your child loses concentration or is restless. This will ensure they want to come back for more!

How to use the book

The same/different

Before attempting the first 10 pages of the book, play matching games with your child. Match shoes, socks, plates, or fruit, concentrating on what is the same and what is different about them.

Talk about things that match.

Talk about what is the same and what is different. Encourage your child to notice small differences as well as the obvious ones. For instance, in a collection of leaves, some may be pointed, others may be round, some rough and others smooth.

This will develop their skill of observation. This skill is helpful in early reading, to differentiate the shapes of letters and how they contribute to words, and in other curriculum areas such as science and art.

Sorting

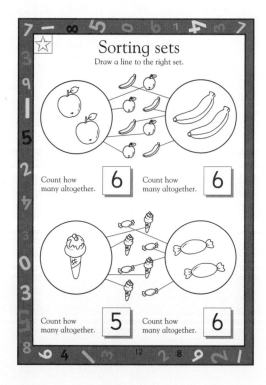

Sorting is a very practical activity, so make sure that your child has many sorting opportunities before doing these pages. Your child can sort the toys at tidying up time, sort the washing, sort the shopping into tins or packets.

Categories or criteria have been used to enable sorting to be both meaningful and useful in everyday life. The pages introduce various criteria which are set in appropriate contexts for your child.

Observation and counting are skills that the child will revisit.

Patterns

Recognising and creating patterns is both fun and an important aspect of a child's development. Later they will be expected to see patterns in numbers and in science results, as well as to recognise the creative element of making patterns.

Before doing the pages talk to your child about patterns that they see all around them. They will probably be on fabric, wallpaper, kitchenware, and in books.

At first let your child copy patterns you have made, with buttons, beads, cups, or even small toys, and then encourage them to make their own. Keep them simple at first, perhaps using just two colours: red button, blue button, red button. As your child becomes more confident, encourage them to create more complex patterns.

It is fun to create your own patterns by printing with corks, small boxes, or with fingers and hands.

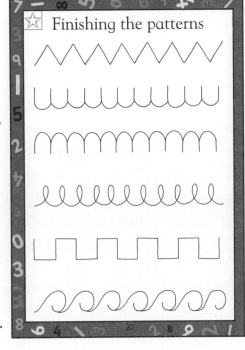

Sequencing

Sequencing and getting things in the right order can be difficult for the young child.

Give your child the opportunity to experience the order or sequence of actions and events within the context of their daily life. Talk about what they do before and after something, and what comes next. Introduce words such as first, second, and third.

Write the numbers 1–10 on some cards and encourage your child to put them in the right order.

Page-by-page notes

Page 2 – Not the same

Your child has to choose the animals that are the same and draw a ring around the animal that is not the same.

At the bottom of the page your child can choose to draw any two animals that are not the same. Talk about their choice.

Page 3 – Not the same

Once again the activity is to encourage your child to find the object that is not the same.

Your child can then draw a sock and a glove that are different from the ones shown on the page.

Page 4 – Different

This page uses the concept of 'different' on its own; the child should by now understand that 'different' means 'not the same'. The child has to draw a ring around the flag that is different, as well as draw the two flags.

Page 5 – Different numbers

This page reinforces the concept of different numbers through the comparison of spots on ladybirds.

Page 6 – Different numbers

The child can count the shapes on the umbrellas and then draw a different amount on the umbrellas opposite.

Page 7 – The same

The child has to identify matching animals. Encourage your child to draw the line starting on the left, moving to the right. This reinforces the left to right movement needed for writing and reading. At the bottom of the page your child can choose the animals they want to draw.

Page 8 – The same

This page introduces the word 'pair'. Talk to your child about pairs – two of a kind that go together. In the second activity, your child can draw a pair of shoes.

Page 9 – The same

This page encourages your child to look at both the size and the type of shape. If they are not sure of their colours they may need your help to complete this task.

They also have to count the number of shapes coloured in a specific colour.

Page 10 – The same

This is a fun page where your child has to match the monsters.

Page 11 – The same

The child has to draw the other half of the monster to match. If it is appropriate, talk to your child about halves. 'Half' is introduced in this context as 'the other half,' which also implies symmetry. Have fun looking for other objects that are symmetrical, buttons, letters, for example. Children can use a mirror to help them see the other half.

Page 12 – Sorting sets

The word 'set' is used instead of group as it is a word with which your child should become familiar before starting school.

On this page the activities involve sorting things into sets by drawing a line to the appropriate set ring, and then counting how many there are in that set.

When your child writes the numbers make sure that they start at the top and that there are no reversals.

Page 13 – Adding to sets

Your child should add to the sets by drawing as many more shapes as asked for and should then count how many in the set.

Page 14 – Sorting the toys

For this activity there are two set rings, one with wheeled toys and the other with toys without wheels. Talk to your child about the toys in the sets. What do they notice? They are all toys, but what is the difference between the two sets? What is the same about the toys in each set?

After you have talked about what your child notices, encourage them to do the sorting. Examples are given for each set.

Page 15 – Sorting the trees

Talk about the page and then let your child do the sorting. For this task your child has to sort the trees according to the number of apples in them. Count how many of each tree. Your child has to draw an additional tree with the requisite number of apples. Now count how many of each type of tree including those drawn by the child.

Page 16 – Sorting the animals

In this activity your child has to sort the animals according to the number of legs and draw a line to the right part of the Ark. An example has been shown.

Page 17 – Sorting the animals

This time the animals with the same number of legs, as specified, have to be ringed.

Page 18 – Sorting the fish

This is both a sorting and a matching activity. Your child has to look at the number on each fish and match that fish to the fisherman wearing that number. They should draw a fishing line for each fish that matches.

Page 19 – Sorting the fish

This too is a sorting and a matching activity. Your child has to look closely at the patterns on the fish and match each fish to the fisherman wearing a hat with the same pattern. They should draw a fishing line for each fish that matches. Children may like to use a different colour for each number.

At the bottom of the page the child has to count how many fish there are of each pattern.

Page 20 – Finishing the patterns

This page encourages your child to finish simple patterns that have been started for them. Left to right movement is important. The first four patterns are the basis for letters.

Page 21 – Finishing the patterns

Your child has to complete patterns and create their own.

This activity can be extended beyond the book and your child can decorate their own paper plates.

Page 22 – Finishing the patterns

Again your child has to complete the patterns. The repeating is simple but make sure your child really looks at the items; some involve counting.

Page 23 – Finishing the patterns

These are more complex, so make sure your child understands what they are to do.

Page 24 – In the right order

This page relates to a child's world and what they do before and after something.

Talk about the pictures before your child puts the ticks in the boxes. Also talk about the pictures illustrating first, second, and third before completing the boxes.

Page 25 – In the right order

The activities involve three pictures and your child has to decide what comes first, second or third in the sequence of events.

Talk about the pictures before your child completes the task.

Page 26 – The missing number

Here your child has to complete the sequence of numbers by drawing the missing objects.

If your child finds it difficult to count in twos, they may need some help with the last activity.

Page 27 – The missing numbers

In these activities there is more than one missing number.

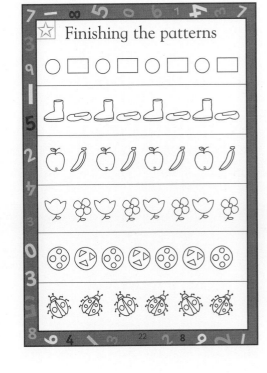

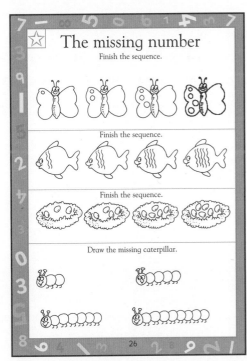

Page 28 – Mary sorted her snails

Your child will have fun matching, looking for patterns, and looking for similarities and differences in Mary's garden.

Children have to sort the different kinds of snails, draw them in the circles given, and count how many snails there are in each circle.

Page 29 – Mary grew some flowers

This page is also an exercise in matching and looking for similarities and differences.

Page 30 – The maze

Your child has to follow the pattern sequence to find their way out of the maze.

Page 31 – Dot-to-dot

By finishing the pattern and completing the dot-to-dot your child will produce lovely pictures.

At the bottom of the page they can then draw their own dot-to-dot pattern.

Page 32 – Teddies

This page is a fun page! The teddy on the right has to be dressed so that it matches the teddy on the left.

At the bottom of the page the child has to dress the teddies the same, using their imagination.

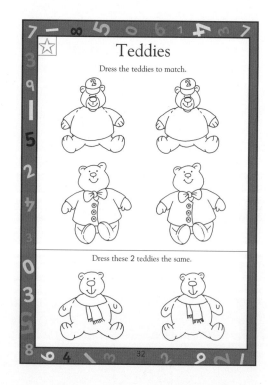

Sorting the animals

Count how many legs.
(Ring) the animals with the same number.

a lion   a bird   a sheep   a fish

| 4 legs |

a fish   a duck   a ladybird   a cat

| 6 legs |

a giraffe   a bird   a lion   a sheep

| 2 legs |

an elephant   a fish   a bird   a mouse

| 0 legs |

17

Sorting the fish

Match the fish to the fishermen.

Sorting the fish

Match the fish to the fishermen.

Count how many fish.

☆ Finishing the patterns

Finishing the patterns

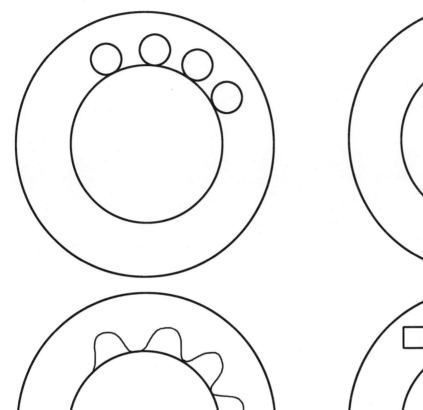

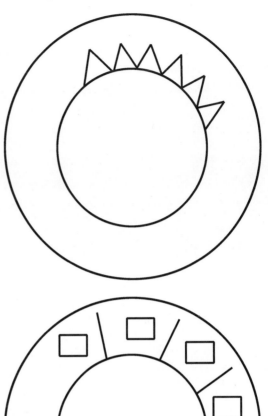

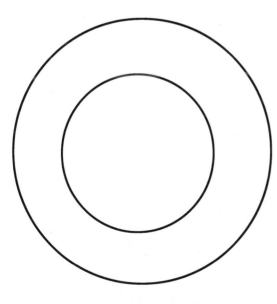

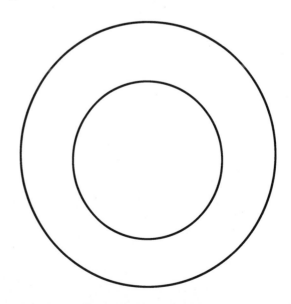

Draw your own patterns.

Finishing the patterns

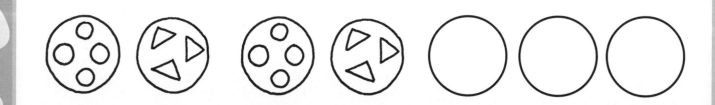

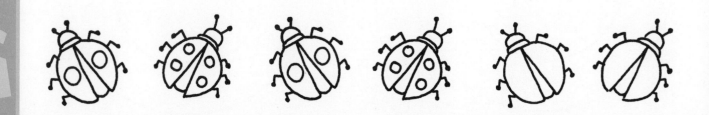

Finishing the patterns

1	2	1	2				

6	7	8	6	7	8			

In the right order

✔ before

✔ after

Write 1st 2nd 3rd in the boxes.

In the right order

Talk about the pictures.
Write lst 2nd 3rd in the right boxes.

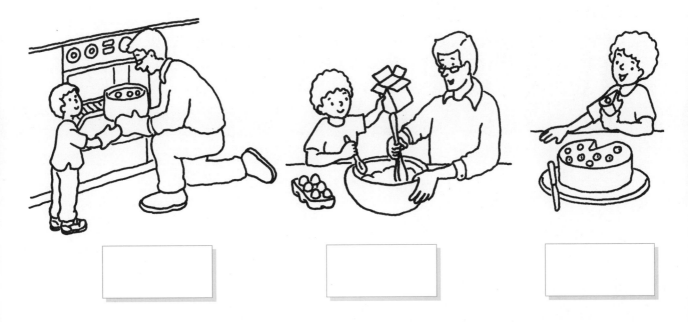

Talk about the pictures.
Write lst 2nd 3rd in the right boxes.

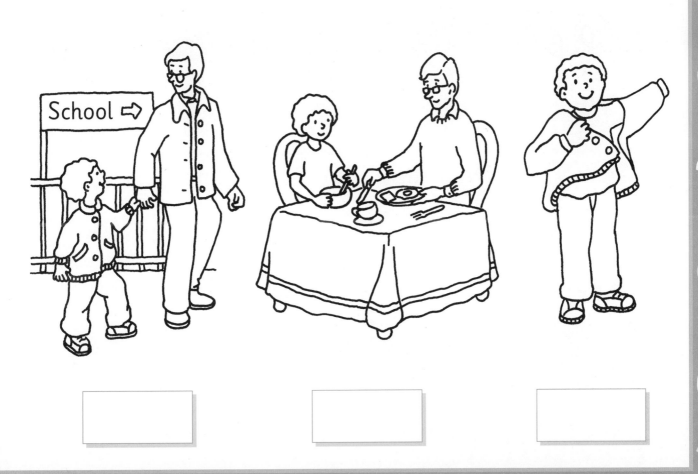

The missing number

Finish the sequence.

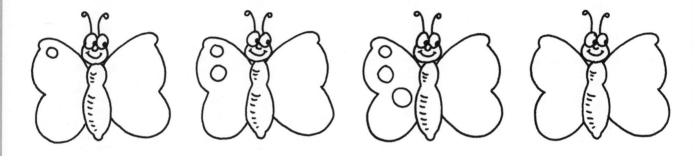

Finish the sequence.

Finish the sequence.

Draw the missing caterpillar.

26

The missing numbers

Write the missing numbers.

Write the missing numbers.

Write the missing numbers.

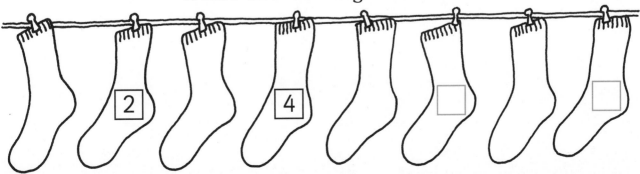

Mary sorted her snails

Sort the snails and draw them in the circles.

Count how many in each circle.

Mary grew some flowers

Draw a ring round the odd one out.

Draw a flower the same.

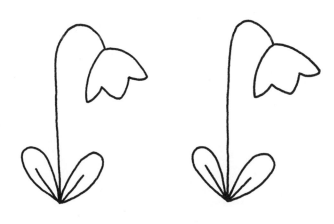

The maze

Follow the pattern to find your way out.

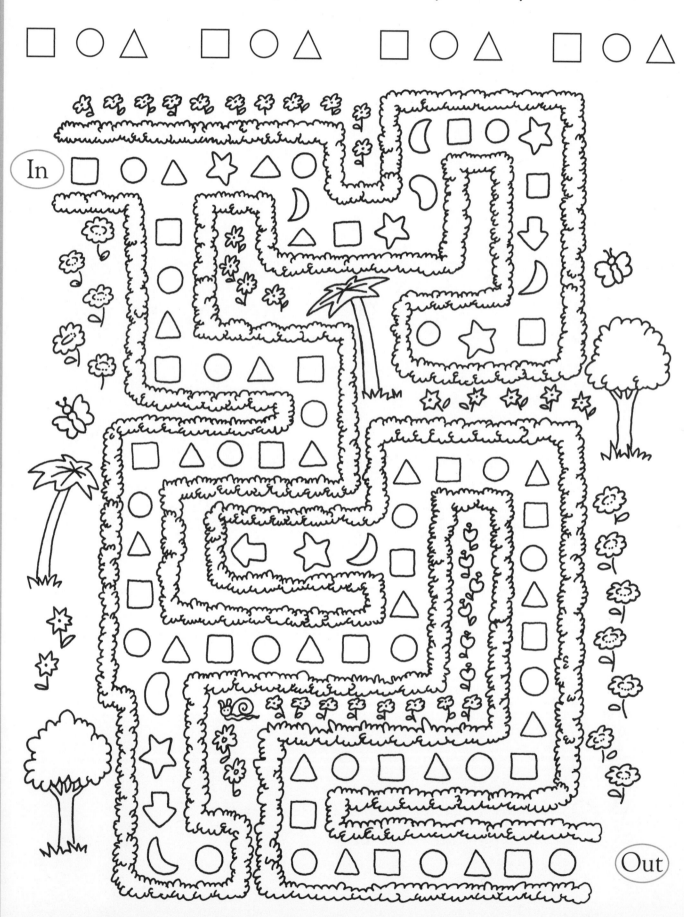

Dot-to-dot

Finish the patterns.

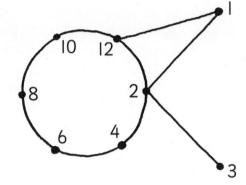

Draw your own dot-to-dot pattern.

Teddies

Dress the teddies to match.

Dress these **2** teddies the same.